# EMPOWERING THE POOR

## Robert C. Linthicum

---

### INNOVATIONS
### IN MISSION

---

Bryant L. Myers, Series Editor

EMPOWERING THE POOR
Community organizing among the city's "rag, tag and bobtail"

Robert C. Linthicum

Published by MARC, a division of World Vision International, 919 West Huntington Drive, Monrovia, California, 91016, USA

Printed in the United States of America. Published 1991. Cover Design: Edler Graphics, Monrovia, California. Typography: Ventura Publisher. Body text: Palatino 12 pts, reduced photographically to 82%.

ISBN 0-912552-75-1

*[The poor are said to be] the rag, tag and bobtail of humanity. But Jesus does not leave them that way. Out of material you would have thrown away as useless, he fashions [people of strength], giving them back their self-respect, enabling them to stand on their feet and look God in the eye. They were cowed, cringing, broken things. But the Son has set them free!*

— Origen (3rd Century, A.D.)

*Empowering the Poor* is the third in MARC's Innovations in Mission series. Other books in this series:

*The Nonresidential Missionary*
*Facing the Powers*

Other books by Robert C. Linthicum:

*Christian Revolution for Church Renewal* (1972)
*Choose You This Day: Creating the Future for Your Church* (1975)
*The People Who Met God* (1980)
*The People Who Turned the World Upside Down* (1982)
*A Transformacao da Cidade* (1990, Brazil)
*City of God; City of Satan: A Biblical Theology of the Urban Church* (1991)

THE 1990S are a time of rapid change in almost every area of life. The political and economic maps are being redrawn. Technology is advancing at a dizzying pace. The center of gravity of Christ's body in the world has shifted to the southern hemisphere. The church is exploding in China and on the Pacific rim. Theology of mission is being written at the grassroots among the poor. The cost of misusing and abusing God's creation is staring us in the face.

In the midst of this climate of rapid change, extreme complexity and almost obsessive pluralism, the church of Jesus Christ is to be in mission. The good news of Jesus Christ and the claims of his kingdom are needed everywhere.

Post-Christian Europe needs to rediscover the gospel that was once central to its culture and sense of being. The nomadic pastoralists—living across the Sahel in Africa, throughout the Middle East, in the eastern provinces of the USSR and in western and southern China—need to hear a gospel "that will fit on the back of a camel." The poor in Latin America need a gospel that restores their relationship with God and reverses the erosion of their quality of life. North Americans need to hear a good news that restores vibrancy of worship and commitment to social change to their culturally captive brand of Christianity. The rich and powerful everywhere need to hear how difficult it is for them to get in the kingdom of heaven.

MARC is in the business of inspiring vision and motivating mission among those who are taking the whole gospel to the whole world. One of the ways we seek to fulfill our mission is to identify and share the stories of innovations in mission which, in our fallible view, make sense in this kind of changing, chaotic world. We seek to broadcast what we have discovered as good news in mission in hopes that others might find this information useful in enhancing their own mission. This series, *Innovations in Mission*, is the tool we have chosen for sharing this information with the global Christian mission community. We hope it will be valuable to mission strategists and executives, mission professors and students, and all those for whom Christian mission is part of living life with Christ.

*Empowering the Poor* is the third book in this series. t addresses the most compelling demographic change affecting mission in the future: by the year 2025 it is estimated that one fourth of the world's population will be living in the squatter settlements in Two Thirds World cities. One in every four human beings will be poor and living in cities with populations over 10 million. How will they hear and see the good news of Jesus Christ?

Answering this question requires we discover answers to a series of very difficult questions. Why are people poor? What does it mean to be poor in the city? How do we go beyond serving the poor and become those who help the poor empower themselves? What kind of strategies result in learning which empowers? What is the role of the church in transforming the cities? How do you develop local leadership that works for and with the poor? Hard questions. No easy answers.

Bob Linthicum, director of World Vision's office of Urban Advance, helps us think through what it means to bring the good news of the gospel to cities such as these. *Empowering the Poor* provides a marvelous series of "how to" stories and illustrations of what churches can do among and with the poor. This book makes concrete Linthicum's theology of ministry in the city described in his recent Zondervan book, *City of God, City of Satan*.

**Bryant L. Myers**
**Series Editor**

# CONTENTS

# INTRODUCTION

EMPOWERING THE POOR has always been the mission of World Vision. This multi-national Christian humanitarian organization has traditionally carried out that mission through childcare, emergency relief, community development, evangelism, and leadership development (both church-related and community-based).

But as World Vision has gone about its diaconal ministry in two-thirds world countries, their cities have been undergoing profound change. Two-thirds world cities are growing at staggering rates due to escalating birthrates and migration from rural areas. Between the years of 1975 and 2000, it is projected that urban populations will have expanded in:

- Africa by 347 percent;
- the Middle East by 302 percent;
- Latin America by 216 percent;
- China by 224 percent;
- the rest of Asia by 269 percent.

In 1950, only seven cities of the world exceeded five million — the population level at which many cities' infrastructure begins to break down as water delivery, sanitation and refuse disposal are strained to the breaking point. In 1985, there were 34 of these huge cities. Twenty-two of them were in the two-thirds world. It is predicted that in less than 35 years, there will be 93 giant cities, 80 of them in the two-thirds world.

The growing size and number of two-thirds world cities levies a toll of human suffering imposed by poverty, overcrowding and disease. Compared to their rural counterparts, the urban poor have worse health problems, suffer more from malnutrition and live in poorer housing, increasing the risk of disease and reducing the chances of recovery.

The pivotal problem of two-thirds world cities is poverty of overwhelming magnitude. Impoverished sectors currently represent between 35 percent and 75 percent of city populations. It is estimated that by 2000 AD, nearly one quarter of all the people living on earth will live in the slums and squatter settlements of cities.

The downward spiral of the two-thirds world city is intensified by the apparent powerlessness of citizens, governments and non-governmental organizations in dealing with these problems. City economic and political structures are overwhelmed by city growth and have only severely-limited resources at their disposal.

In countries where another religion is dominant, the church is a small and relatively powerless presence. As a minority community, the church is splintered, cautious and centered upon survival.

Most important to World Vision, people of the slums and squatter settlements believe they have little control over their surroundings, their future or their economic state. Their greatest sense of poverty is not the lack of money or property, but the lack of power. The people believe they lack the essential ingredients necessary for them to bring order, dimension and structure to their lives.

Over the past decade, it has become increasingly clear to the leadership of World Vision that this rural- and village-based organization had to begin concentrating ministry in the world-class cities of the two-thirds world. But, obviously, the simple transfer of its relief and development programs into the political, social and economic complexity of the city would not work.

Therefore, in 1988, World Vision created the Office of Urban Advance to enable World Vision to effectively undertake its mission and ministries among the urban poor. Since then, Urban Advance has focused on three mission objectives.

- **Empowering.** Any urban ministry which does not enable the poor to directly deal with their own problems will not really deal with a city's overwhelming needs. World Vision's Urban Advance pulls churches and the poor together into coalitions that empower the people to solve their slum's deepest social, economic and political problems.

- **Equipping.** More than 90 percent of the pastors in many two-thirds world cities have neither theological education nor practical training in urban ministry. The Urban Advance equips pastors for more effective urban ministry. This is done by building city-wide networks of support and by conducting urban training events which provide both a biblical framework and practical strategies for urban ministry.

- **Evangelizing.** It is the ordinary Christians already present in a city who are best equipped to share God's Good News in that city. The Urban Advance provides proven

strategies by which pastors and local churches can share
the gospel at the point of people's needs.

The Urban Advance is currently working in 28 cities in 16 countries
in Asia, Africa and Latin America. It works with the churches of each city,
as they seek to reach out to that city. And it works in the worst slums and
squatter settlements of those cities, seeking the empowerment of the very
poor.

Community organizing is the primary strategy World Vision uses
to join with the two-thirds world urban poor in their empowerment.
World Vision employs and trains community organizers who move into
the slums and live among the people. There, they follow the principles
enunciated in this book in working with the indigenous leadership of their
slum to take charge of that community. This relief and development
organization is now doing community organizing in 40 urban slums
around the world.

The principles of social analysis, networking and community organizing are also taught to urban pastors in the cities and slums where
World Vision is at work. That training then becomes the backbone of those
pastors' effective equipment in ministry among their city's poor. Community organizing is therefore central to all that World Vision seeks to do in
the city.

Because of the strategic place community organizing plays in
World Vision's urban strategy, and because of the place training has
played both in empowering the poor and the church to be effective in the
city, we decided to produce a book on World Vision's approach to
community organizing. This book is the result.

It is our hope that this resource will be of help both to communities
of the urban poor and to church leaders as they seek to work for the
empowerment of the people in the great cities of both the first and the
two-thirds world. Consequently, we pray that this book will be of support
to you as you seek to be faithful to God's call to you in your city.

*Robert C. Linthicum, Los Angeles*
*May 5, 1991*

# ONE

# Why are so many urban people poor?

IT WAS 1957, and I was working among black teenagers in a slum in a large city of the United States. Our youth ministry included a spectrum of recreational and athletic activities centered around Bible studies. A fourteen-year-old girl (whom I will call Eva) began to attend one of these Bible study groups.

Eva was an exceptionally beautiful teenager, physically mature for her age. She became even more radiant when she received Christ as her Lord and Savior. I began discipling Eva, building her up in the "nurture and admonition" of the Lord.

My academic year was drawing to a close and I was looking forward to returning home for summer vacation. Just before I was to leave my teenage "parish," Eva came to me greatly troubled.

"Bob," she said, "I am under terrible pressure and I don't know what to do. There is a very large gang in this slum that recruits girls to be prostitutes for wealthy white men in the suburbs. They are trying to force me to join them. I know it's wrong. But what should I do?"

I gave Eva all the appropriate advice I had learned in church and college about how if she resisted evil, it would flee from her. I urged her to stick with her Bible study group and not to give in to this gang's demands.

Then I left for my summer vacation.

Three months later, I returned to school and to the ministry in which I was engaged in that city. Eva was nowhere to be found. When I asked about her at the Bible study, the other youth told me she had stopped coming about a month after I had left.

I went to Eva's home. She answered my knock on the door. As soon as she saw me, she burst into tears.

"They got to me, Bob," she said. "I've become a whore!"

"Eva, how could you give in like that?" I unsympathetically responded. "Why didn't you resist?"

"I didn't give in," she responded. "I was forced." Then she told me a story of terror.

"First, they told me they would beat my father if I didn't become one of their 'girls.' I refused, and they beat him—bad. Then they said my brother was to be next. He ended up in the hospital. Then they told me that if I didn't yield, they would gang-rape my mother. I knew they meant it, and I had no alternatives. So I gave in and became one of their whores."

"But, Eva," I said, "why didn't you get some protection? Why didn't you go to the police?"

"Bob, you honkey," Eva responded. "Who do you think are in that gang? It's the police—the police are running the prostitution ring!"[1]

## Why are people poor in the city?

The poor are a vast populace within the cities of the world. By the close of this century, more than 20% of all the people on the face of the earth will be the urban poor. One out of every five human beings will live in cities and be profoundly poor. And half of them will be children.

The number and sorry condition of the urban poor in both the first and third worlds is staggering. In Bombay, India, alone, a million people live in a slum built on a giant garbage heap. On the other side of the Indian sub-continent, between 500,000 and 750,000 Bengali live their entire lives on the streets of Calcutta—never once to experience a roof over their heads.

In Detroit, 72% of all the young employable adults in that city's poorest census tract can't find work—and probably never will hold a job. In São Paulo, Brazil, 700,000 children have been abandoned by their parents to live by their wits on that great city's streets.

Fifteen thousand of Manila's street children survive through prostitution. Forty thousand children are prostitutes in Bangkok, Thailand— their primary customers being Americans and Japanese. Sixty percent of the entire population of Guayaquil, Ecuador, live in shantytowns amid garbage-strewn mud flats and polluted waters.

Fifty thousand homeless people live on New York City streets. Another 27,000 live in temporary shelters. Seventy-five percent of the families who live in Lagos, Nigeria, live in one-room shacks. More than a million people—50% of the city's population—live in the giant slums of Mathare, Korogocho and Kibura in Nairobi, Kenya. In reality, between 35% and 75% of the population of most third-world cities are poor.[2]

---

1    Robert Linthicum, *City of God; City of Satan: A Biblical Theology of the Urban Church* (Grand Rapids, MI: Zondervan, 1991), pp. 45-46. Used by permission.

2    Statistics gathered from original research done by the Office of Urban Advance, World Vision International, and from the following sources: *Stemming the Tide of*

What it is terribly important for us as Christians to realize is that behind every statistic are millions of individual stories, stories of poverty, of sickness and despair, stories of people who are unable to influence the course of their own lives and are powerless to change the course of their neighborhoods or cities.

Bob Pierce, the founder of World Vision, once prayed, "Let my heart be broken with the things that break the heart of God." How heartbreaking is it for the poor in the cities?

I spent an afternoon in a slum of beggars and thieves within easy walking distance of downtown Medellin, Colombia's second-largest city. I had been visiting families in that slum, fourteen to twenty-five families to a house. I was ushered by one very pregnant woman into her apartment —an apartment only large enough to contain just one bed and boxes piled in the corners. There on the bed lay this lady's 1-1/2 year old child, her nine-month-old baby—and the woman was seven months pregnant.

"Every day," she told me, "I carry my two babies into downtown Medellin. I lay my two babies out on a blanket, sit next to them and open my coat so everyone can see how pregnant I am. And then I beg for money. All the money I get to raise these babies, I get from begging this way."

How heartbreaking is it for the poor in the cities? I was escorted into a vest-pocket slum of 2,000 in Nairobi, Kenya. The mud-and-wattle slums of African cities, with dirt roads and streams of open sewage, are bad enough. But in this slum, my eyes were met by total devastation. The roof of every house was gone, the smell of smoke was heavy upon the air, and the single room of each house was charred and covered with the litter of collapsing beams and thatch.

"Last night," a spokesman of those squatters told me, "government police entered our slum. It was pouring rain. They told us they were there to evict us. We have been here for more than 25 years, and they have never bothered us before. But now they were going to make us get out. They made us leave our houses, our families standing in the rain. Then they made the men of the slum set fire to the roofs and to all the contents of their own homes; if we refused to do it, they beat us and threatened to shoot us. We were helpless to resist."

How heartbreaking is it for the poor in the cities? Several years ago, I walked down Falkland Road in Bombay—the famed red-light district of India. As I walked block after block, I was stunned by what I saw.

*Displacement* (Coalition for the Homeless, 1986); Patrick McAuslan, *Urban Land and Shelter for the Poor;* Gerald Luedtke and Associates, *People in Faith United Neighborhood Revitalization Plan* (Detroit, 1985); Lester Brown and Jodi Jackson, "Assessing the Future of Urbanization," *State of the World* (1987), The Population Institute, Washington, D.C.

Falkland Road is lined with alcoved buildings. In each alcove, curtains have been hung and a bed or mat placed. Outside each alcove stands a prostitute, waiting for business. These prostitutes line both sides of the street, block upon block, scarcely seven feet apart—scores and scores of prostitutes, as far as the eye can see.

What most shocked me about these prostitutes, however, was their age. Easily one-third of them were flat-chested little girls who had not yet reached puberty. All but one of the hundreds of prostitutes I saw that day looked like they were under 16. And around their feet and on their laps played swarms of little children—some no older than my grand-daughters—consigned in turn to become male or female prostitutes in just a few more years.

This is the city—for God's sake! This is the city into which the poor are flocking, forced to live lives that break God's heart and should break ours, as well.

Why are there so many poor people in the cities? If city life is so difficult, why do people continue to move to the city? There are two forces which create such large populations of the poor in the city: migration and reproduction.

First, reproduction. As the population of the very poor in the city escalates, that rapid growth is fueled by the inevitable cycle of birth and new life. The population of Seattle, Washington, for example, is reproduced every year in Mexico City—as many babies being born in that city as there are migrants entering that city each year.

Whereas the increase of poor in first world cities is primarily due to reproduction, the increase of poor in third world cities is due primarily to migration (as it was in first world cities 50 to 100 years ago).

People move to the city both because they are "pushed" out of rural and village areas, and because they are "pulled" by a city's allure.

They are "pushed" into the city because of rural disasters, country blues, landlessness and urban ideology. Disasters such as wars, floods and crop failure force people into refugee camps which are often on the outskirts of major cities. Governments tend to support city-based industries while ignoring rural needs. Consequently, young people see better opportunities for education and advancement in the cities.

Landlessness also forces people into the cities. Export crops such as tobacco, coffee and tropical fruit favor big farmers who can afford labor-saving mechanization, fertilizers and high-yield seeds. Small tenant farmers can't compete; they end up losing their land and have to go to the city to look for work.

Finally, the country is seen as backward and dull, an image now common with the global spread of consumer culture. Everyone knows someone from their village who has made it "big" in the city, and they honestly believe they can replicate his success.

But people are also "pulled" to the city as well as being pushed out by their rural conditions. The allure of the city was very graphically captured in that old post-World War I song, "How 'Ya Gonna Keep Them Down on the Farm After They've Seen Paree!" There are four major forces that pull a person to the city.

First, freedom—people who feel hemmed in by tradition and rigid customs come to lose themselves in the crowds and the permissiveness of the city. Second, bright lights—cities appear more exciting and glamorous; they attract the bored, the lonely, the ambitious and the adventurous.

Third, work—wages are higher and jobs seem more plentiful in the city. Living costs are higher too, but the possibility of paid work and of constantly remembering the village example who "made it big" in the city is a powerful lure. Fourth, better living conditions—city families may live in slums and squatter settlements, but they are usually closer to clinics and hospitals and have easier access to electricity and piped water than their country cousins.[3]

Thus it is that the poor flood to the nearest large city, pushed off their land by economic, political and social forces far bigger than themselves, and pulled to the city by its seductive allure. They all come, believing that they will discover incomparable wealth, health and happiness there. And they end up, instead, moving into the slums and squatter settlements where others from their village or region live. They look for non-existent work, and finally end up in the first world going on to welfare or in the third world creating their own jobs—selling soft drinks at a football stadium, wiping clean the windshields of cars stopped at a traffic light, making and selling trinkets on the sidewalk or begging, picking pockets or stealing. They come to the cities with great hope, and soon run into the city's cold despair. And so they become people of despair themselves.

But why are these migrants and babies poor? Why do the poor in the city seem to stay poor—sometimes, for generation after generation? Those who are financially secure or politically powerful like to suggest that it is the fault of the poor that they are poor. Those who have been amply rewarded by the reigning system of the city and country like to suggest that the poor are lazy, lack education, lack personal initiative, have too many babies, etc. In other words, they suggest that it is their own fault that the poor are so poor; they are simply inferior people.

---

3    "Cities — the Facts," *The New Internationalist*, December 1987, p. 17

Now, of course, some poor are lazy, lack personal initiative and think only of today (but so are some middle class and rich people). But are these the *causes* of their poverty? Or are these the inevitable *result* of being powerless?

## Poverty and power

To truly understand the condition of poverty today, one must understand how power is exercised in the city. Poverty is not so much the absence of goods as it is the absence of power—the capability of being able to change one's situation. It is because one is already severely limited in what he or she can do to change one's plight that one becomes impoverished. Marginalization, exploitation and oppression are not simply results of poverty, but its primary causes.

A great deal has been written analyzing the causes of urban poverty. These social analyses range from Marxism on the left to laissez-faire capitalism on the right. Each social theory purports both to understand the primary causes of poverty and to offer the ideal solution to such poverty.

But perhaps one of the most profound and comprehensive analyses of power—and perhaps one of the most ignored, as well—is found in the Bible. That study analyzes how power is used in the city—both its legitimate and illegitimate exercise—to maintain the establishment or to liberate the poor. And because that exploration can include the spiritual dimensions of power, that biblical explanation of power can (and does) examine the nature, origins and eventual denouement of the use of illegitimate power. This makes the biblical analysis far more profound than any secular study of the subject undertaken today.

Our exploration on empowering the poor must begin by understanding how power is exercised in the city and how it produces the poor. That study we will undertake by examining the Bible's analysis of power.

When I discovered that it was the police who were running the prostitution ring into which Eva was forced, I had come face-to-face with the nature of evil in my city. The police—the very people entrusted by society with the task of protecting and defending the people—were, in reality, the worst exploiters of the people. I eventually discovered that what the police were doing in that one precinct was only the tip of the iceberg in that city. The entire legal and political system of that city was arrayed to protect a mass betrayal of the people to enable police, judges and politicians to enrich themselves at the people's expense.

It was in this encounter in 1957 that I first realized that a city's evil is far greater than the sum of the sin of its individuals. The very systems of a city could become corrupt, grasping, oppressive, and exploitative. I realized that sin in the city was systemic and corporate. And it little mattered if all the Evas among a city's poor were to be converted, because the evil in the systems could destroy them through their corrupting corporate power. If the church does not deal with the systems and structures of evil in the city, then it will not effectively transform the lives of that city's individuals.[4]

Understanding the nature of evil in the city requires examining the primary systems that make a city function and then analyzing these systems biblically.

What are the classic systems of a city—that is, the systems any city *must* have in order to function? It is widely suggested that the systems that order the life of a city are economic, political and religious. By "religious" I mean the system that gives the city its reason for existence (the word's original sense, from the Latin *religio*, means "to bind fast" or "to structure"). A religion is that which structures or brings ordered meaning to life. With such a definition, we can readily see that even the most secular and materialistic city has a religion, because it uses a commitment to modernity or communism or technology or nationalism to bring order and structure to its existence.

All other social institutions (education, health care, culture and the arts, social services) are subsystems of the economic, political and religious systems of a city. In fact, until several hundred years ago, each of these subsystems was regarded as a part of the religious system, for it was the responsibility of the church to carry out these services and to be patron of the city's art and culture.[5]

What insights can we gain from Scripture to help us understand these urban systems and the condition of poverty that results?

**The city as city of God**

It is a great surprise to discover that the Bible has a great deal to say about the systems and structures of human society. It is because we approach the Bible with a highly individualistic perception of Christian faith that we miss the biblical writers' corporate and systemic analysis of human society. Yet grasping that analysis enables the church to move in liberating and society-transforming ways in the city. We can only lightly review that analysis in these pages, but I have written elsewhere in detail on this topic (*City of God; City of Satan: A Biblical Theology of the Urban Church* [Grand Rapids, MI: Zondervan, 1991]), and if you desire to explore this topic to greater depth, I would commend that material to you.

---

4   Linthicum, *op. cit.*, pp. 46-47.
5   Ibid., p. 47.

The Scriptures present us with a description of what the structuring systems of society ought to be like. The political, economic and religious systems have been created by God, the Scriptures teach us. They were created to enable humanity to structure their life together, to thereby create the city a paradise for all, and thus to bring glory to God.

What did God intend the political, economic and religious order to be? The book of Deuteronomy—as are the last four books of the Pentateuch—is given over to the answering of that question. A good example is Deut. 6:4-19.

> *Listen, Israel: Yahweh our God is the one Yahweh. You shall love Yahweh your God with all your heart, with all your soul, with all your strength. Let these words I urge on you today be written on your heart (Deut. 6:4-6).*[6]

> *Do not follow other gods, gods of the people around you, for Yahweh your God who dwells among you is a jealous God; his anger could blaze out against you and wipe you from the face of the earth. Do not put Yahweh your God to the test as you tested him at Massah (Deut. 6:14-16).*

God has created the religious system of any unit of society— family, neighborhood, religious community, city, state—in order to enable that people to know and love "Yahweh your God with all your heart, with all your soul, with all your strength." The religious system was created by God to enable the people to be in continually vital relationship with God. For the religious system to be used for any other purpose—to enable the people to follow any other gods (i.e., power, prestige, possessions, parochialism)—will not be tolerated by God.

> *Let these words I urge on you today be written on your heart. You shall repeat them to your children and say them over to them whether at rest in your house or walking abroad, at your lying down or at your rising; you shall fasten them on your hand as a sign and on your forehead as a circlet; you shall write them on the doorposts of your house and on your gates (Deut. 6:6-9).*

> *Keep the commandments of Yahweh your God and his decrees and laws that he has laid down for you, and do what is right and good in the eyes of Yahweh so that you may prosper and take possession of the rich land which Yahweh swore to give to your*

---

6    All biblical quotations are taken from *The Jerusalem Bible* (Garden City, NY: Doubleday and Co., 1966), unless otherwise noted. Used by permission.

*fathers, driving out your enemies before you; this was the promise*
*of Yahweh (Deut. 6:17-19).*

God has created the political order of each unit of society—
whether family or empire—in order to enable that unit to live life in a
structured, ordered and predictable way. The political system is meant to
derive its authority and power from a leadership which is living, both
personally and corporately, in a close relationship with God. Such relationship will inevitably be practiced in the way that leadership structures
the corporate order of that society. This can be done only by creating a
political structure which does "what is right and good in the eyes of
Yahweh so that you may prosper." The political order God requires for
all human society, therefore, must be an order of justice.

> *When Yahweh has brought you into the land which he swore to*
> *your fathers Abraham, Isaac and Jacob that he would give you,*
> *with great and prosperous cities not of your building, houses full*
> *of good things not furnished by you, wells you did not dig,*
> *vineyards and olives you did not plant, when you have eaten these*
> *and had your fill, then take care you do not forget Yahweh who*
> *brought you out of the land of Egypt, out of the house of slavery.*
> *You must fear Yahweh your God, you must serve him, by his*
> *name you must swear (Deut. 6:10-13).*

And what is a Godly economics? The economics of the society God
would build through his people, is an economics of grace. A recurring
theme throughout the Old Testament is that the Jewish people own
nothing. The land and its possessions are not theirs to do with as they
would please. It is a gift from God, "cities not of your building, houses
full of good things not furnished by you, wells you did not dig". All of
life is a gift from God. Therefore, those who are responsible for the
economic maintenance of a society must be committed to its stewardship.
The wealth is not an individually-owned wealth; it is a "common wealth"
—a wealth belonging to everyone because it ultimately belongs to God.
Therefore, the task of those who manage that wealth is to be good
stewards of it, maintaining and using it for the common good.

What, then, did God create the systems of the city to be? He created
the *religious system* of the city in order to bring and maintain the people
in a vital relationship with God.

If that relationship was both individually and corporately dynamic
enough, that would have a profound impact upon the way that city would
handle its *politics.* Because every city dweller would be a child of God, it
would be the responsibility of those who would manage the political
process to seek justice and equitable treatment for all.

Such a commitment to justice would then profoundly affect the way that city would go about managing its wealth. Its *economic system* would exist in order to care for and increase the "common wealth" of that city—practicing an economics of stewardship and equitable distribution for all.

A religion of Godly relationships, a politics of justice, an economics of stewardship—this is what the biblical writers perceived was God's agenda for the city. This was how God designed the systems of the city and of the state to function, both for the well being of humanity and for the glory of God.

### Systems gone awry

But one would not describe the city of today as a city centered in the worship of God and practicing a politics of justice and an equitable stewardship of resources for all. If anything, most cities are the exact opposite. What has gone wrong? And why has it gone wrong? How does the Bible describe the systems of a city as they are practiced today?

The Bible is full of analysis of systems gone awry. The conflict between Pharaoh and Moses is actually a conflict around political and economic repression. The economic corruption of the Israelite empire by Solomon and the sorry story of the kingdoms of Israel and Judah from Rehoboam to Zedekiah is the painfully long illustration that it is easier to take people out of the (Egyptian) empire than to take the empire out of people.

In the story of Daniel we see a power-crazed Nebuchadnezzar, who on a whim brought unbelievable oppression on Hebrew youth. The story of Nehemiah is actually the story of a people rebuilding both their city's walls and their corporate life in the face of significant political and economic opposition.

Or we can observe the political might of the Roman Empire joining forces with the economic power of the Jewish religious institution in the time of Jesus to hold the common people in thrall while justifying such exploitation by appealing to Jewish religious nationalism.

Again, we can turn to the time of Paul and view the urban churches he founded struggling against Roman power, the self-serving of Greek and Near Eastern religions and a matrix of Jewish and gentile local and international economic interests.

One of the clearest statements about systems gone awry, however, is made by the prophet Ezekiel in his condemnation of Jerusalem. In chapter 22, Ezekiel castigates Jerusalem for the unbelievable corruption to which it has yielded.

> *The word of Yahweh was addressed to me as follows, "Son of man, are you prepared to judge? Are you prepared to judge the murder-*

*ous city? Confront her with all her filthy crimes! Say, 'The Lord Yahweh says this: City shedding blood inside yourself to bring your hour [of destruction] closer . . . you have come to the end of your time'" (Ezek. 22:1-4a)!*

What has caused Jerusalem—once the city of God—to become such an evil city that God must destroy it? Ezekiel lists the contributing factors to that city's hellish descent in what has to be one of the most brilliant social analyses that appears in the Bible.

*The word of Yahweh was addressed to me as follows, "Son of man, say to her, 'You are a land that has not received rain or shower on the day of anger, and whose princes are like a roaring lion tearing its prey inside her. They have eaten the people, seized wealth and jewels and widowed many inside her'" (Ezek. 22:23-25).*

First, the *political system* (the "princes") of Jerusalem has become overwhelming oppressive. Called by God to preserve justice and order in the city, Jerusalem's political leaders have instead given themselves over to the oppression of the people. And for what purpose?—so that they might "seize wealth and jewels" and increase their political and military might. Their lust for power has corrupted the political establishment's exercise of their God-given responsibility to maintain justice equitably for everyone.

*Her leaders in the city are like wolves tearing their prey, shedding blood and killing people to steal their possessions. People take bribes for shedding blood; you charge usury and interest, you rob your neighbor by extortion, you forget all about me—it is the Lord Yahweh who speaks (Ezek. 22:27, 12).*

Second, the *economic powers* (the "leaders") have become the exploiters of the people. Given by God the responsibility of maintaining the "common wealth" for the good of all, the keepers of the city's purse have used their position to exploit the people. They have stolen the people's possessions, Ezekiel tells us. They have charged unfair interest and cheated in their business dealings. And this they have done for one reason and one reason alone—to gain as much wealth for themselves as they could and thus to build their own estates.

It is critically important to recognize that there is a finite amount of the "common wealth." There are only so much economic resources available to any city at any given time. Therefore, the only way the managers of that wealth can gain a disproportionate amount of that wealth is to take it from those who lack economic power. Instead of viewing the city's wealth as a shared wealth which they have the responsibility to wisely manage for the equal benefit of all, they begin to perceive the wealth as theirs for them to handle as they see fit. The more they accumulate such wealth for themselves, the more they find ways to deprive others of that wealth. And thus occurs the inevitable growth of a lower class of people who have neither the access to wealth nor the knowledge of how to use that wealth. And thus a class of the impoverished are created because of that increasing inequitable distribution of the "common wealth."

> *Her priests have violated my Law and desecrated my sanctuaries;*
> *they have drawn no distinction between sacred and profane, they*
> *have not taught people the difference between clean and unclean;*
> *they have turned their eyes away from my sabbaths and I have*
> *been dishonored by them (Ezek. 22:26).*

Third, the *religious leaders* (the "priests") have become controllers of the people. Whereas the economic powers of a city can exploit the people to gain control of a city's wealth, and the political powers can coerce the people into submission through laws designed to protect that wealth, it is the religious system which can truly exercise control over the people. It exercises that control by shaping the belief system and values by which the people interpret and understand their life. Therefore, if the religious system endorses the political and economic establishment as good, the people will tend to accept that endorsement. This phenomenon is exactly what Ezekiel is describing here.

Israel's religious leaders were assigned by God the responsibility of introducing the people to God. It was their task to maintain the people's relationship to God. If Israel was to have a vital faith experience with God, that would only come through the faithful conduct of the prayer, practice, proclamation and presence of the religious community as it would lead the people into relationship with God.

But what did Israel's religious leaders do with that great privilege? First, they themselves have broken their own personal relationships with God, "violating my Law and desecrating my sanctuaries". Second, they have withheld from the people the instructions the people needed for them to practice their faith rightly before God. The result of such withholding of the faith has been that the people "have turned their eyes away from my sabbaths and I have been dishonored by them."

And why did Jerusalem's religious leaders withhold knowledge of God from the people? Simply because they were interested only in building their own power and wealth by controlling the people and the people's response to the political leaders and economic structures of their city. The priests controlled the people, and they were amply rewarded for doing so by the king and the controllers of the public purse.

Thus, Ezekiel lays out how the systems, created by God to bring order and justice to human institutions, become corrupted by evil. The economic system, created by God to manage the people's "common wealth," instead claims that wealth for itself and sets itself to the goal of increasing its own wealth; this it accomplishes by exploiting the people.

The political system, fiscally dependent upon the economic system, slips from the maintenance of a system of justice to creating a system of order, controlling the growing impoverished class by laws and the might of military or police who oppress the people.

Finally, the religious system is called upon to justify this increasing rape of the people by using its role as keeper of the values of that city to control the people rather than to lead the people to authentic relationship with God.

Therefore, a system created by God to bring humanity into relationship with God, and through that relationship to create a politics of justice and the nurturing of the "common wealth" becomes a system of economic exploitation and political oppression which uses the values of the community to control and oppress the people.

But Ezekiel is not yet through with his social analysis. He continues on in his exploration of the forces which changed Jerusalem from the city of God into the city of Satan.

> *Her prophets have whitewashed these crimes with their empty visions and lying prophecies. They have said: Yahweh says this; although Yahweh has not spoken (Ezek. 22:28).*

What can call the economic, political and religious powers of a city or a nation to accountability? In Israel, God created the office of *the prophet* to accomplish that task. The prophet stood outside the establishment, neither beholden to them nor in anyway economically dependent upon them. It was the task of the prophet to cry, "Thus says the Lord" to the people and systems of power, demanding of them that they fulfill the responsibility given them by God. This was the essential task of Isaiah, Jeremiah and Ezekiel, of Amos and Micah and Hosea.

But when the systems of a city become corrupt enough and corrupting enough, when a city sinks spiritually, politically and economically far enough, when oppression and exploitation and control become the order of the day, what happens to the prophet? He becomes seduced by these systems. His critical voice is stilled.

The great lesson from the prophets in the latter years of Jerusalem's pre-exilic existence was the struggle that went on between the "true prophets" and the "false prophets" (e.g., see Jeremiah 28). The struggle was this: the false prophet was speaking words of peace and assurance to the economic, political and religious leaders, and consequently, justifying their actions before the people. The true prophet was calling the king, priests and business leaders to accountability for the way they were misusing their assigned role, and doing so purely for their own personal aggrandizement.

The sign that the systems of a city are becoming truly corrupt is whether the voice of the prophet is being stilled. In the old days, the prophet's voice was stilled by cutting off his head. Today, the systems are much more sophisticated; they simply seduce the prophet with money or power.

But the degradation of the city is not yet complete. Ezekiel continues his analysis:

> *The people of the city have taken to extortion and banditry; they have oppressed the poor and needy and ill-treated the settler for no reason. I have been looking for someone among them to build a wall and man the breach in front of me, to defend the city and prevent me from destroying it; but I have not found anyone. Hence I have discharged my anger on them; I have destroyed them in the fire of my fury. I have made their conduct recoil on their own heads—it is the Lord Yahweh who speaks (Ezek. 22:30-31).*

When the systems descend from evil to ever-greater evil, when they give themselves over to exploitation, oppression and control in order to cement their own power, when those who call the systems to accountability become seduced by those systems so that there is no longer a voice of opposition to be sounded, then will come the greatest corruption of all. *The people* will be corrupted.

The last great hope for a nation or a city is its people. Abraham Lincoln well understood this when he said, "God must love ordinary folk, because he created so many of them!" A nation or a city is only as good as the integrity of its people. Revolutions come from the people precisely because of their integrity—precisely because they are able to discern right from wrong, justice from oppression, law from order—and are able to say, "This is wrong, and we won't stand for it anymore!"

But when the systems, corrupted by evil, corrupt the city enough, even the people are seduced by those systems. They finally begin to accept for themselves the standards the systems have built their empires upon. They cannot accrue the economic or political power of the systems. But the people will learn their lessons well from those systems. They will turn on each other. Exploited and oppressed by the systems, the people will become exploiters and oppressors of each other. And with their exploitation of each other (whether through violence or drugs or crime or crack), the last hope for redemption of the city dies.

What, then, must God do to the city so thoroughly corrupted? Ezekiel gives us the answer.

> *You have [become] an object of scorn to the nations and a laughingstock to every country. Near and far, they will scoff at you, the turbulent city with a tarnished name. . . . I mean to disperse you throughout the nations, to scatter you in foreign countries, and to take your foulness from you. I shall be dishonored by you in the opinion of the nations; and so you will learn that I am Yahweh (Ezek. 22:4-5, 15-16).*

**Systems above systems**

This does not complete the analysis of a city's systems, however. The most profound social analysis of the city came from the Apostle Paul as he sought to prepare his churches to survive in a Roman dictatorship.

Paul suggested that there is a level of evil in the city which goes beyond its systems and the people who occupy those systems. There is a spiritual dimension in the victimization of the poor and the power-accruing activity of the systems. If we do not understand that spiritual dimension, then we are bound to repeat the excesses of the systems. If we do not appreciate the spiritual dimension of the struggle, then the oppressed, once overthrowing their oppressors, will inevitably become the new oppressors of a new victim people. And the reason this is true is because the problem is not simply a systemic problem or a people problem—it is a spiritual problem.

The struggle in the city, Paul suggested, is not simply against "flesh and blood"—the city's systems and the occupants of those systems. The struggle is against "the Sovereignties and the Powers who originate the darkness in this world, the spiritual army of evil in the heavens" (Eph. 6:12). There is a Power that is at work behind the powers; there are spiritual forces committed to evil that are infiltrating and using the systems and structures to capture that city for the Evil One. The political, economic and religious systems are the structural forms (created by God) which are invaded and used by demonic powers to corrupt and destroy all that is good in that city (1 Pet. 3:22; Col. 1:14-20).

What is St. Paul trying to describe here? He is recognizing what Ezekiel recognized before him—that a city is more than an accumulation of buildings and people, more than systems exploiting, oppressing and controlling the poor. A city has a spiritual dimension to it. In fact, it *is* a spiritual reality.

The Bible uses a particularly graphic way of describing this reality. It suggests that every city has an angel "brooding" over it and protecting that city (Rev. 2-3; 2 Kings 19:35-36; Deut. 32:8-9; Dan. 10:1-11:2).

Now that might seem hard for people in the twentieth century to adopt. But we should not allow our secular scientific framework get in the way of perceiving the truth that people like Paul and Ezekiel, Jeremiah and Jesus were communicating pictorially to a story-telling people.

I believe that what the biblical writers are telling us is that everything in life—a family, a church, a neighborhood, a city, a nation—has a spiritual dimension to it. The political system of a city consists of more than its people, electoral processes, structures and institutions. That system is infused with a spiritual essence; it has unimagined and unexplored inner depths that are its "soul." The angel of a city is the inner spirituality that broods over the city. That spirituality has immense power, either for good or for ill. And if the church seeks to do ministry or if the poor work for their own liberation in that city without understanding and dealing with that spirituality, they are destined to be seduced or crushed by that Power. That is why a chief task of the organizing of a community is not simply that of "organizing" (either to throw the rascals out or to gain power for the people). It is to work at creating a new "community" of people who love God and their neighbor as themselves.

This, then, is the adequate answer to the question, "Why are there poor people in the city?" This completes our analysis of the powers and Powers that maintain control and set direction for a city.

Why are there poor people in the city? It is not because they are lazy, uneducated, or lack initiative. It is because they lack power. People are poor because other people are rich—and use their wealth and power to control the poor. The poor are victims of such power, and as victims, often turn to victimizing each other.

What, then, can be done? How can the poor become the people God created them to be? How can the systems and structures work for justice, maintain the "common wealth" for all and seek to bring the whole city into vital relationship with God—rather than to seek to economically exploit, politically oppress and spiritually control the people? How can the city work authentically for a Godly community no longer dominated by the powers of darkness which corrupt every effort of humankind?

It all begins with working for the empowerment of the poor.

# TWO

# Empowerment through community organization

HOW CAN THE CHURCH EMPOWER the poor? The very way we ask a question reveals a great deal about the assumptions we bring to an issue. For example, the above question is the wrong question. I would be immediately suspicious of anyone who posed that question that way. Why? Because such a question reveals that the person asking it neither understands the nature of empowerment nor what are appropriate or inappropriate roles for the church to play in its ministry with the marginalized, oppressed and impoverished around it.

### The church in the city

There are three distinctly different responses that any church or mission organization can make to its city. The response the church chooses to make decides whether that church will play a significant role in the poor's empowerment, will provide social services out of its largess or will simply ignore the needy around it. What are those three responses which are either liberating good news or stifling repression to the city's poor and powerless?

The first response of the church to its city is to see itself as being *in* that city and *in* its community. It does not feel any particular attachment to that city. It does not particularly identify with the community. It is simply physically present in that community. That happens to be where its bricks and mortar meet the ground. It may have no particular relationship to the people of that community.

Now, often a church that sees itself as "in" but not "of" its community will have had in earlier days a significant commitment to that community. That church may have been created as a parish church, a church of that specific neighborhood. But then the neighborhood began to change and decay. As that neighborhood began to deteriorate, the people who had lived in that neighborhood and who went to that church began to move out. So, increasingly the church becomes a commuter congregation with people traveling into the city and into that neighborhood in order to attend the church, but whose lives are lived out in another community. The result is that they have no stake, no psychological ownership in that community. To be a church *in* the city is the first response of the church with regard to the city and to its neighborhood.

### The church to the city

The second response is for a church to perceive itself as a church *to* the city and a church *to* the community. In due time, many churches following the scenario I just described, will begin to realize that if they do not interact with their geographical community in some way, they are going to die. If the church is to live, it will have to find some way of reaching out to its neighborhood. So the church begins to become concerned about its city, its neighborhood and its problems. This, of course, is a much more holistic approach because of the recognition that the church must be present to the people around it and must be concerned both with evangelism and social action. It is inadequate to be concerned with the souls of the people around the church—particularly if those people are poor—unless the church is also going to be concerned about the social and economic needs of the people.

There is great potential in this kind of approach but there is also a fatal flaw. The Achilles heel of this approach is the perception that the church knows what is best for that neighborhood. Those Christians look at that neighborhood and say, "Look at all these poor people here; what these people need is a youth program for their teenagers to get them off the streets." The church says, "Look at all these children running around the streets here; they have no place to play. What the church needs to do is to develop a program for those children." Or the church looks at the number of senior citizens sitting on their porches and it says, "What our church needs to do is to develop a ministry to senior citizens."

Do you see the common element there? The common element is that *the church decides what is best* for the community. A primary assumption of effective urban ministry is to recognize that the people who are best able to deal with a problem are the people most affected by that problem. The people best able to deal with teenagers who are running amok in their neighborhood, for example, are the people who live in that neighborhood.

Now, although that seems self-evident, that concept is one of the most difficult insights for Christians to apply. We can understand it intellectually, but it is extremely hard for us to implement that perspective in our own ministries.

The reason why is that the church operates out of the unbiblical assumption that, because we know the gospel, we know what is best for that community. Therefore, we undertake ministry in that community out of our "definitive" understanding of the needs of that community ("what this slum needs is a child-sponsorship, health care and family education program"). This, in turn, robs the people of that community from the responsibility of dealing with their own corporate issues.

The fate of any program or project developed under such assumptions is inevitable. It will function successfully only as long as the church or mission agency is willing to commit its people, money, materials and buildings to the program. But "burn-out" will eventually happen. And once programmatic exhaustion has occurred, so that the well-intentioned pastor or mission executive can no longer raise sufficient money or resources or workers to maintain that program, it will die. And it will die because it has never been a project of the people. They never perceived it as their program, but rather a program of the church or mission agency. And because the people have no ownership in the program, they will always remain spectators and clients of it, never participants and goal-owners. Therefore, its death is inevitable.

It is not appropriate for the church—in fact, it is strategically a very bad thing—to look at its community and decide what it needs to do to that community in order to change that community. It is not appropriate because that approach is to perceive the community and its people as an object to be ministered to and the church as the subject—the only viable change agent in that community. Such an attitude is actually colonialist in nature, and reveals a paternalistic attitude toward people.

**The church with the community**

The third response of the church in the city is to be the church *with* the city. There is a profound difference between being a church *in* or *to* an urban neighborhood, and being a church *with* its neighborhood. When a church takes this third approach, that church incarnates itself in that community. That church becomes flesh of the peoples' flesh and bone of the peoples' bone. It enters into the life of that community and becomes partners with the community in addressing that community's need. That means the church allows the people of the community to instruct it as it identifies with the people. It respects those people and perceives them as being people of great wisdom and potential. Such a church joins with the people in dealing with the issues that the people have identified as their own. That is the approach in which the most authentic urban ministry is actually done.

The third response of the church—to be the church *with* the people of its neighborhood—is an approach which enables the church to join with the people in addressing the issues of that community, but doing so from the recognition that the only people who in the final analysis have the capability to change that community and to deal with its problems are the people of that community. The church comes alongside them and supports them and works with them in that endeavor, sharing with those people the particular gifts and strengths the church has to contribute to that situation. It is that body of Christ which identifies with the people, casts its lot with the people, works along with the people. But it cannot and will not do the people's work for them. Only the people can assume responsibility for their own empowerment.

Now can you see why the question, "How can the church empower the poor?" is the wrong question? It is the wrong question because no one can empower anyone else! Only you can take charge of your own situation. The task of the church is not to empower the community. The task of the church is to join the empowerment of the community—to participate in it, to be an integral part of it.

As we can see from this exploration, there are three essential responses of the church to the city.

- First, it can ignore the city and the needs of the people around it as it fixates on preserving its own life. It can view itself as a fortress.

- Second, it can provide social services and do good works for and to the people in the city. It can view itself as the savior of the community.

- Third, it can join in the community's struggle to determine for themselves what kind of community they want to have, a community with justice for all. The church can view itself as a partner with the community.

The task of the poor in the city is empowerment. The unbelievable living conditions of the urban poor—wretched jerry-built housing, polluted water supplies, open sewers, a lack of balanced food, terrible health conditions—are essentially manifestations of a far deeper problem. For the primary problem is a distribution of power. A few have considerable wealth and political clout—and back up that clout with the laws of the state, their control of the city's economic machinery, and often with military hardware, guns, police dogs and even tanks. Unless the poor can find ways to effect an economic and political redistribution of power, all the efforts to feed, house and clothe them will only be palliatives that will never significantly change their estate.

The task of the poor in the city is their own empowerment. And the task of the church is to come alongside the poor, both becoming their advocates before the rich and to join with the poor in their struggle to deal with the forces that are exploiting their community. The most effective means for bringing about such empowerment in the city is community organization.

Community organization is a uniquely urban approach to Christian ministry among the poor. Modern cities are the centers both of great power and utter powerlessness, of absolute poverty and corrupted wealth. And it is in the midst of such power and wealth, vulnerability and poverty that the church makes its home.

Community organization is the process by which the people of an urban community organize themselves to deal corporately with those essential forces that are exploiting their community and causing their powerlessness. The church's place in such organizing is to join with the poor to take responsible action to identify and deal with the forces that are destroying that community.

How World Vision goes about doing this in an urban slum is particularly instructive. Each of the field offices interested in participating in World Vision's Urban Advance draws up its own strategy, identifying the slum communities in which it will organize, and contextualizing the generic urban strategy of this development agency.

Acting as a "mid-wife in the birth of a community," trained World Vision community organizers move into a selected slum or squatter settlement, live there and work among the poor and the churches for three to five years. Focusing on that slum, the organizer follows a five-step process:

- **Networking:** The organizer visits and befriends the people, identifying key issues and leaders while building trust between the poor and the churched.

- **Coalition-building:** The organizer gathers the poor and Christians together into coalitions to address community needs identified by the people.

- **Acting/reflecting/acting:** A dynamic process begins. Coalitions reflect, act, evaluate, act again and reflect more deeply. Reflection includes a freedom to look at their own sinfulness and gospel solutions. The results? Root problems are addressed, systemic action taken. Self-confidence and community trust are built. And Christians who have joined with the poor in addressing these issues can naturally share their faith.

- **Leadership empowerment:** Coalition leaders inevitably surface, are identified and equipped. Church leadership integrated with the community also emerges and is trained. Support networks emerge among coalitions as a vision for the birth of a community unfolds. Community-wide leadership results.

- **The birth of community:** The slum people begin taking charge of their situation as the result of problem-solving coalitions. The community is organized, the church becomes integral to community life, and the poor are empowered. Under such community organizing, the slum's quality of life radically improves and the people increasingly take charge of their own lives and of their community.

### A cup of cold milk—the liberation of a neighborhood

The scenario which we have just explored sounds like magnificent theory. But I would like you to see this liberating philosophy at work in the story of the organizing of one small *favela* in a medium-sized city in Brazil—Natal.

Natal is a city of over one million in the poverty-stricken northeast region of Brazil. World Vision Brazil is working for the empowerment of the poor in the slums of Natal. The following story was shared by our community organizer there—a profound example of the empowerment of a desperate slum community.

To truly appreciate this story, the reader needs to be aware of two factors. First, it is the policy of the Brazilian government that all urban slum children are to receive milk daily, which is supplied through redeemable milk tickets. Second, the urban slums of Brazil are officially organized by the government around neighborhood-sized residents' associations which then, in turn, belong to a district-wide community council.

Here, then, is the story of the liberation of a Brazilian urban slum through a cup of cold milk, as told to me by the World Vision organizer in that community:

"I had been visiting with the people in one favela, talking with them wherever I found them. While I was visiting, I became terribly thirsty. I went to a small snack bar in the favela, and I ordered a soft drink. Then something interesting happened. A small child came up to me, and asked me to buy for him a glass of milk. Then I thought to myself, 'But doesn't the government distribute milk?' So, I asked of the bar owner, and he replied, 'Here the community is very large. And the community council is distributing these milk tickets just for a part of the community.'

"Then I noticed that the group had grown even bigger. And I began talking to them all, 'What are you doing to solve this situation?' They replied, 'We can do nothing, because the community council is the only group that can distribute the milk tickets, and our leader is fighting with the other leader.' And I told them, 'Do you know what the basic problem is?' And they replied, 'We don't know.' 'The problem is,' I replied, 'that it's not their milk to do with as they please. It's our milk—given to us by the government. Why should we let them decide how to distribute our milk?' Then I proposed we make a group of five to go to the house of the president of the residents' association.

"So we went there, and we waited for him. After quite a while, he arrived, and wondered why so many people were there. Then I asked him, 'Why are these people—who represent so many families—not getting the milk tickets?' And he told me, 'The problem is, I am the enemy of the president of the council. And the politician who provides the tickets to him for distribution is his friend. He doesn't provide those tickets to me.'

"Then I asked him to set a meeting with the residents' association, and he agreed. When the meeting occurred, we were very excited because there were so many people there, because everybody was interested in getting the tickets. Then I raised this question, 'How many times did you get together to solve this problem?' And they replied, 'Well, as unbelievable as it seems, this is the first meeting we have had on this subject!'

"Then we talked about what we could do, and a gentleman gave an idea. 'Why don't we go to talk with the secretary of health (a governmental regional administrative post)?' The crowd selected the people, representative of the community. But how could we get to the secretary? As we talked about it, someone in the group indicated that he was acquainted with the secretary. And we invited a neighborhood pastor to join us; he is someone whom many of the people trust. We set a meeting date, and we went to the secretary's office—ten community residents, the resident association's president, the pastor and me.

"We met with the secretary, who was impressed by the size and makeup of the delegation. He told us he had never received a visit like this, and he wanted to know what the problem was. The residents told him the problem. He was very frustrated, because he didn't know his aides were acting like this. He promised to solve the problem.

"But the delegation insisted that they wanted a public meeting with the health secretary in the community. He accepted the challenge, and came to the meeting. We invited all the heads of all the mothers' clubs, and all the community's residents to attend, as well.

"Before our public meeting was to be held, our delegation went into the community of the politician withholding the tickets. We asked the people whether they were happy to know that they were getting our milk tickets while we had none. They said, 'That's not fair, but we can do nothing.' We replied, 'What do you mean, 'you can do nothing?' You can talk to the politician who supplied you with the tickets. You can explain to him everything that has happened, and our anger.'

"Soon the politician came to see us. He defended himself, of course, and blamed the man above him. 'He's not willing to distribute the tickets to the other side. So, I can do nothing,' he said. And we told him, 'If you can't do it, we will elect someone who can get something done!'

"We said we wanted him to attend the public meeting that the health secretary would be attending. He was fearful. But we said to him, 'If you do not go, we will tell the community you didn't want to come to clarify the problem. They will never vote for you again.' At the meeting, he was there.

"The public meeting began, and the people quickly began expressing their frustrations. And the health secretary invited all the leaders of the mothers' clubs and the residents' association to speak their mind. And after they were done, he said, 'Beginning next week, we will begin distributing the milk tickets. I will keep checking with you to be sure the milk is reaching the people. And from now on, not only your residents' association, but the mothers' clubs and the other clubs will receive the tickets to distribute to the families. And inspectors will check regularly with the leaders to receive any other complaints about health or food distribution.' And the head of the community council began releasing the tickets.

"This brought a very positive aspect because people began speaking out and standing up for their rights. I then said to them, 'If you could solve the milk problem, why can't you meet with the other side of the community and together solve some greater problems?' Thus, our association got together with the community council. And there was great fellowship, so that there were families who had members who belonged to the association and had also members of the council. And they began to realize we could accomplish more working together than working against each other. So they started to become happy, because of that. So both the residents' association and community council began having meetings with the community, to listen to the community.

"In the larger district, there was a group of very poor people who had moved into the favela and had taken possession of some available land. They had done so because their land had been taken over by a land development company, and they had been expelled from it. When this problem was told at our community meetings, all the people thought this was unfair. So the community got together. Even people who were not directly involved in the problem joined the displaced ones. So we went to the governmental housing agency. Again, we had a delegation of ten people. But the agency's director wouldn't receive us. Then we returned the next week with fifteen people, but he didn't want to receive us.

"What were we going to do? One woman said, 'If he doesn't receive us in his office, we'll have breakfast with him in his house!' So twenty people got together, and at 7:00 in the morning, while he was still asleep, we gathered in front of his house and began clapping our hands. It is a well-to-do district, and the neighbors became fearful, asking, 'What's going on? What's happening? Let's go to the police because they are planning to invade this man's house!' But the police had been notified by us about what we were planning to do. They had agreed we could meet. So, when the residents complained, the police did nothing.

"Then we rang the bell. The man was awakened, and then he said, 'I can't receive you now.' But he promised that he would receive the group in the afternoon at his office.

"When we met, he set a thirty-minute time limit on us. But we ended up staying four hours! He got involved in the case. He saw the possibility of going to the area, and he said he would send someone to go and check the situation. One of our people prepared the documentation so that we could get the government to give the land to the squatters. An engineer studied and reported to the government what would need to be done to make the area safe and sanitary for the people to live there. And the land became the home of these squatters.

"Through our visiting in the community and our involvement of the churches in dealing with the problems the people identify as important, we have seen some beautiful changes. The churches are getting involved in the problems of the community. The people of the community are becoming aware of the churches. Through this work of ours, some district associations are changing, working for the common good rather than simply for their own purposes. The people have a new optimism about themselves, and are feeling good about their favela. And through the people's growing power, many politicians are committing themselves with the pastors in a more direct way to the people. Even the president of the community council, who was considered an agitator, is now a fervent Christian. We have attempted to do the work, not just for the people but with the people, because the people are coming out with their own projects. They know their own realities and we don't want to do anything that interferes with their dealing with their own realities."

As you can see from this story of the empowerment of a Natal slum, this strategy is a proven strategy. It is proven, not just in World Vision, but in countless communities through both religious and secular organizations all over the world. It is a strategy that creates trusting community among previously suspicious city people. It enables the local church to incarnate itself in its barrio, just as Jesus did in Jerusalem. And it enables the poor to help themselves—not by relying on others, but by identifying their own problems and implementing their own solutions together.

**We can't save the city, but . . .**

We can make a difference! The church should approach its urban ministry with a sober awareness of the overwhelming predicament of the poor and of the exercise of power in today's cities. The strategy expressed above does not guarantee that in some magical way the church will transform the sin, greed and injustice of the city. Such evil will resist all attempts to exorcise it.

The urban strategy presented in this book simply provides a framework in which to do city ministry. It is a strategy that is designed to empower the poor, to equip the church and to evangelize those who do not know Christ. And it does so by enabling the church to become partner and messenger to the people by joining with them in action at the point of the people's deepest pain.

# THREE

# Community organization:
# what it is and how it differs
# from development

WHAT IS COMMUNITY ORGANIZATION? How does it work? How does it actually empower the poor? And what does it have to do with the work of the church in the city?

Community organization is that process by which the people of an urban area organize themselves to "take charge" of their situation and thus develop a sense of being a community together. It is a particularly effective tool for the poor and powerless as they determine for themselves the actions they will take to deal with the essential forces that are destroying their community and consequently causing them to be powerless.

The assumption upon which community organizing is built is that "united we stand; divided we fall." It recognizes the tremendous power generated by people acting collectively. Particularly, the poor and powerless of a city—whether in the first, second or two-thirds worlds—are excluded from full participation in the social, political and economic life of their city. Community organization empowers them to meaningfully encounter, cope with and sometimes change these urban structures and systems. But only if they act collectively!

The organizing of a community occurs around the continuous use of the process of reflection and action. Reflection enables the people to identify both the systemic causes and their personal attitudes and actions which have led to their powerlessness. It provides the means for continually evaluating the actions the people take to address these causes and attitudes.

But words without action are meaningless rhetoric. The process of reflection and action also provides the opportunity to take concrete, specific actions that come out of their reflection. These actions are always undertaken and developed by the people themselves. And no action is complete unless its results are analyzed by the people and inform both their corporate reflection and their next actions.

Because it is an organization of people collectively addressing the issues of their neighborhood, a community organization has the following characteristics. It is:

- **Relational**, based upon the development and maintenance of one-to-one contacts out of which mutual risk and trust grow.

- **Pragmatic**, acting locally and doing what the community identifies as needing to be done in that community;

- **Winnable in the actions it takes**, carefully selecting its issues so that people experience success in the early stages of the organizing effort, making its actions realistic in scope;

- **Democratic in its decision-making**, including all the groups (both formal and informal) and peoples in that community in the decision-making process;

- **Developmental**, committed to a process of discovery and action, rather than following "canned" programs and procedures;

- **Seeking structural changes**, not preoccupied with direct service for the needy of its community (although some direct service may be an integral part of a community organization's program), but concerned with giving people power to make decisions so that systems can be changed.

- **Consciousness-raising**, thinking globally and systemically about issues;

- **Leadership-intensive**, not staff-intensive; a primary part of staff's job is to awaken, develop and train the natural leaders of the community to assume effective leadership of that community;

- **Pro-active**, rather than reactive; with a long-term vision for that community, the organization can decide the issues they will address rather than react to the decisions and actions of the politically, economically or religiously powerful;

- **Initiative-seizing** rather than being defensive; it anticipates what will happen next and acts upon that anticipation. In that assertive action, it is not afraid to confront the "principalities and powers" of its society;

- **Value-based rather than issue-based**; the community organization acts from the standpoint of faith, vision and conviction in its commitment to that community; it is not established around single issues like housing, economic development, health care, and so on.

## Comparing community organization and development

Community organization is often seen as something distinct from community development. In reality, there are many similarities. Both community development and community organizing have the same essential objective—the empowerment of people, so that they can assume responsibility for their own community.

Community organization is actually a further stage of empowerment than is development. Its difference with development is a difference in degree, rather than in kind. The two differ as follows:

- **Long-term**: Community organizing is oriented toward a long-term approach to development, one which is concerned to build a force for the self-determination of the people for the life of that slum or squatter settlement; traditional community development is medium-term in duration.

- **Inclusive**: To be truly successful, community organization must include as many formal and informal groups in a community as possible; it is, in reality, an "umbrella" organization of that community; this would include groups of diverse and even opposing ideologies.

- **Responsive**: A community organization concentrates on identifying its issues and actions out of the pain and frustration of the people; it will therefore not plan or manage by objectives to the degree that community development would.

- **Action orientation**: A community organization reflects participatively only in order to determine the actions it needs to take against its common-identified foes; it is not primarily process-oriented as is community development nor program-oriented as is a project.

- **Confrontive**: A community organization has a very realistic understanding of power, including the recognition
  that there are no permanent enemies and friends. It recognizes that often the only recourse open to the people is
  to confront those who are choosing to be enemies on a
  particular issue. Many community development groups
  view confrontation as intimidating and seek to cooperate
  with those in power; such cooperation can often lead to
  the group being seduced by those in power.

- **Staff**: Community organizing staff has one primary job
  —that of working with the people to organize themselves
  to set and carry out the agenda the people determine is
  necessary to make their community self-determining. No
  community organizer should ever assume the role of
  project director. If community organizing is truly effective, it should require a very small staff (usually no more
  than one or two organizers) who ought to eventually
  work themselves out of a job (especially in the two-thirds
  world).

- **Permanent structure**: Truly effective community organizing will lead to a permanent organization of the people,
  an institution which will remain the focus for the power
  of the people in that community for decades to come—no
  matter who moves in or out of that community. Traditional community development projects do not necessarily create long-term institutions representing the interests
  of the people.

Community organization is community development adapted to
the city, a peculiarly urban approach to dealing with the concentrations
of economic and political power in the city as well as large bodies of the
poor and powerless. It is significant that, whereas community organizing
has proven the most effective development methodology in cities over the
past fifty years, it has not been as commonplace in rural and village
settings.

### Why the urban church should be involved

But what does the church have to do with community organization? If community organization is the process of mobilizing the poor in
a given slum or squatter settlement to take responsibility for their situation, what place does the church have in that? And what does this have
to do with the gospel?

The unique power of Jesus Christ in his work of redemption among us was that he became one with us. Our God was not an absentee God who demanded that we come up to God's expectations. Rather, the Scriptures tell us:

> *[Jesus] did not cling to his equality with God but emptied himself to assume the condition of a slave, and became as we are; and being as we are, he was humbler yet, even to accepting death, death on a cross (Phil. 2:6-8).*

When Jesus sought to win humanity to God, he became one of us, lived among us, voluntarily took upon himself our limitations, and "was humbler yet, even to accepting death . . . on a cross."

That is exactly what Jesus calls the church to be and do in the city. If we are to win the city's poor for Christ, we will do so only as we become one with them, live among them, voluntarily take upon ourselves their limitations and join with them in addressing our common problems and issues. That is what the Bible means by "incarnation;" that is the imitation of Christ to which God calls the church in the city. The very essence of urban ministry is for God's people to identify with the needs of the poor and powerless and to join with them in bringing about biblical justice.

In the third century A.D., the pagan Celsus and the Christian Origen engaged in a debate on Christianity. In the course of the debate, Celsus reportedly declared,

> *When most teachers go forth to teach, they cry, "Come to me, who are clean and worthy," and they are followed by the highest caliber of people available. But your silly master cries, "Come to me, you who are down and beaten by life," and so he accumulates around himself the rag, tag and bobtail of humanity.*

Origen's response to Celsus' attack ranks as one of the most profound statements ever made about the power of Christianity. He replied,

> *Yes, they are the rag, tag and bobtail of humanity. But Jesus does not leave them that way. Out of material you would have thrown away as useless, he fashions [people of strength], giving them back their self-respect, enabling them to stand on their feet and look God in the eye. They were cowed, cringing, broken things. But the Son has set them free.*

This is the work to which the church is called in the cities of the developed, developing and undeveloped worlds. This is the ministry it needs to have to the broken, the poor, the lost in the slums and squatter settlements of our giant cities. To enable people to free themselves from being cowed, cringing, broken things. To enable the poor to regain their self-respect. To support people as they fashion themselves into people of pride and dignity out of material exploiters would use and then throw away. In the name of Christ, to unbind them and to let them go free! This is the work of the church in the cities of the world. And community organization gives to the church the means to undertake that ministry—not only in rhetoric, but in the action that liberates a people.

# FOUR

# Urban work which empowers

ACCORDING TO WEBSTER'S DICTIONARY, something that is "normative" establishes a standard. What are the standards upon which urban ministry which empowers are built? There are five normative presuppositions upon which everything else in both urban ministry and community organization rests.

1. *Only the poor of the city can assume responsibility for solving their own predicaments.*

The only people who can deal with a problem are the people who are most affected by that problem. What do I mean by that?

When I was pastoring a church in Detroit, my teen-age son was getting himself into a lot of trouble. He was drinking, not getting his schoolwork done and was running around with a rather rough group of friends. Those first three years of his high school life were absolute hell for my wife and me. It was during that period that I went to see a very close friend of mine. When I began to share with him my concern and my heartache about my son, he said to me something that seemed at the time terribly cruel. But I later came to realize the wisdom in what he said.

He said to me, "Bob, I can listen with concern to what you have to say. I can weep with you. I can even feel great pain for what you are going through. But I cannot solve your problem for you. There is only one person who can deal with your son's alcoholism, and that is your son."

What is obviously true for a marriage or in a family situation is equally true for a community or a neighborhood. The people who are most capable of solving a severe community problem are the people of that community. No one else, not even the church, can know what is best or assume responsibility for an urban community.

The essential poverty of the city's poor is powerlessness. Poverty in a city of the third world is not so much the absence of goods or of money, as it is a marginalization of the poor, their economic exploitation and political oppression by the powerful. Because there is only a finite amount of wealth in any country, the powerful can monopolize a majority of it only by denying it to the poor. And such denial is done by depriving them of any significant economic and political power.

When the church becomes aware of such urban poverty, its tendency is to undertake programs to meet the discernible manifestations of such powerlessness—hunger, unsanitary conditions, polluted drinking water, slum housing. In doing so, the church has determined what the problems of those slum communities are, selected the solutions for these problems and undertaken the projects to address those issues.

What the church does not realize in undertaking such ministry is that it is contributing to the problem, not solving it. It is addressing a result of the people's powerlessness, and not the essential problem itself— aggrandizement of the poor by the rich and powerful. And it is contributing to the people's powerlessness because rather than working with the poor as the poor seek to address the root problem, the church is making the poor dependent on the intervention of the church. People may be fed, water made clean, sanitation systems installed, housing built—but the people are still without self-determination. They are therefore more helpless than before, for they have been made dependent. They have been treated as objects for care, not self-determined and capable subjects of their own destiny.

Only the poor of the city can assume responsibility for solving their own powerlessness. And the church must find ways to support and encourage the actions of the poor to assume control over such powerlessness, rather than contributing to it by encouraging greater dependency.

## 2. The poor can be empowered only by acting collectively through reflection, projects, and actions.

The second normative presupposition is that people who are excluded from full participation in the social, economic and political life of their city or of their neighborhood can be empowered to participate when they act collectively. As long as people assume responsibility for their community, but assume that responsibility individually, they will be unsuccessful in significantly changing the course of their neighborhood. If people can be empowered to work cooperatively, to work as a single unit, then they will be able to take responsibility for the life of that community and consequently, to participate fully in the life of that city.

There have been two kinds of power through history—the power of money and the power of people. One of the realities of life is that the power of money often wins battles, but rarely wins the war. Every revolution has been the result of collective people power.

The power of the poor emerges from collective action. It must also come through reflection, when the people take time to think about what is happening to them and why. Nehemiah, for example, led the people of

Israel through reflection about the political, economic, and religious forces depriving them of their rights.

Reflection can be acted out in projects or in actions. *Projects* are activities that people do to deal directly with their problem—like an economic development project. *Actions* are the people's demand for a legally appropriate response from the government that they are not receiving. But whether the people's response is action or projects, it is the collective response that truly empowers.

3.  *The body of Christ in a city can best carry out ministry to that city.*

To believe that urban ministry can be carried on by denominations or mission organizations based halfway around the world is ludicrous. The key question is what would happen to such a ministry if for some reason the denomination or mission organization was forced to leave the country? The answer to that question reveals both the vulnerability of an outside organization and the inherent weakness of having a ministry centered in anyone other than the local people.

If an external mission organization becomes an advocate for the poor and confronts systemic evil, its position in the city may be threatened. The day may come when the government will no longer be willing to have such an organization in their cities. Consequently, the essential task of any foreign mission organization is to equip local leadership. Anything other than that is Christian colonialism.

The issue is essentially a theological issue. Does God adequately equip and prepare those whom God has called for ministry? It is my firm belief that God has already placed in every city of the world and is calling forth the leadership that God wants to carry out ministry in that city. God does not leave his church bereft of leadership. Nor does God make the church dependent upon outside leadership; for that to happen is to leave the church in a dependent and vulnerable stance—as helpless as are the poor, the oppressed and the marginalized of the city.

The truth of this normative presupposition is given vivid illustration in the Chinese church. When mainland China fell to the Communist revolutionaries in 1949, Chinese Christians numbered under 3,000,000. Persecuted as reactionary and capitalist, the church was purged of its western influences. All foreign missionaries were driven from the country and Chinese Christians who remained outspoken for their faith were hunted down and executed. To protect itself, the church was driven underground.

Forty years later, as the face of Communism softened across China, the church began to emerge from hiding. And what greeted the world was overwhelming good news. The church which had entered into persecution and was stripped of its foreign organizers had, in those forty years of persecution, grown from its pre-revolutionary 3,000,000 to a movement numbering close to 50,000,000. The Chinese church thrived only when Chinese Christians assumed responsibility for its secret ministry to China's powerless and lost.

God has placed in the city's body of Christ and has called into being all the leadership that city and church needs. If there is an external denomination or mission organization in that city, its task is to help equip that leadership for ministry, to come alongside them and strengthen them in their work—and then to get out of the way! It is only upon such ecclesiastical self-determination that God's church can proclaim a gospel which has credibility in the eyes of the people, be relevant to the issues and struggles of the people it is seeking to reach (especially the poor and powerless), and be secured against persecution.

4. *The church can assume its local mission only through proclamation, ministry among and with the poor, and focusing that ministry in empowerment.*

Traditionally, the church acts out its calling in the city through its presence, prayer, practice and proclamation.

The church is called to be God's presence in the city. Jeremiah instructs the Jews brought as captives to Babylon to "build houses, settle down; plant gardens and eat what they produce; take wives and have sons and daughters" (Jer. 29:5-6a). In other words, he is asking God's people to enter fully into the life of the city—even a heathen city to which they have been exiled—to enter into its economics and make a contribution, to make an investment of themselves and their families in that city. The church and its people are called to become God's presence in their city, and by living and moving and having their being there, to bless that city by simply *being* the children of God.

The church is also called to pray for the city. Psalm 122 calls on God's people to "pray for peace in Jerusalem" (verse 6). And one prays for the city's peace by praying for its poor and oppressed, its economic conditions and for political justice, for those city dwellers who do not know either God or their filial relationship with God's people (verses 6b-9).

The church is called to practice its faith in the city. God's people are called to work for the good of their city, "since on its shalom your shalom depends" (Jer. 29:7). One works for a city's peace by working for its health care, sanitation, environmental issues, housing, employment, its provision of social services (Isa. 65:18-25). But in all their actions, the people of God practice their faith by their acts of compassion toward the oppressed, the provision of social services and contending for social justice.

The church is also called to proclaim in the city its faith in Christ. The words of Jesus at the inauguration of his ministry describes the breadth of the church's proclamation in the city—"good news to the poor," "liberty for captives," "new sight for the blind," "freedom to the downtrodden"—the gospel shared with everyone (Luke 4:14-22).

The end result of the church's presence, prayer, practice and proclamation in the city ought to be the liberation and empowerment of the city's poor (both spiritually and materially). The church's calling in the city should be acted out in such a way that the powerless and marginalized are supported and motivated to assume responsibility for their own situations—and to take such action corporately. If the "cowed, cringing, broken" people of the city are not set free in Christ through the church's presence, prayers, practice and proclamation, then the church is not doing the job for which God called it into the city. The mission of the urban church should result in the spiritual and physical empowerment of the city's "rag, tag and bobtail."

If these four principles are true, what remains as the task of a denomination, ecumenical body or para-church organization?

5. *The task of the para-church organization, denomination or mission group is to support the local body of Christ in whatever ways will more effectively enable the church to undertake ministries of empowerment with the poor.*

The external mission organization exists to be a servant to the body of Christ which God, in God's wisdom, has placed as witnesses in that city. The para-church organization exists to equip and motivate the church by teaching, by supporting and by example. Such enablement needs to include the following:

- Engaging the city's pastors and spiritual leaders in continuing biblical and theological reflection about the city, so that they develop their own urban theology contextualized to that specific urban environment;

- Carrying out empowering ministries among the poor as laboratories for community organizing and urban evangelism;

- Providing support and training to urban pastors so that they both understand and are motivated to carry out urban ministry *with* the city, rather than *to* or *in* the city;

- Partnering with churches in specific slums and squatter settlements to work with the poor in the people's collective efforts to address their own issues;

- Becoming advocates for the city's poor and powerless both in front of that city's or country's systems and structures of power and before the western world's economic and political systems which benefit by the maintenance of the status quo in that country;

- Using their influence with the city's powerful, the city's systems and structures, those of other religions and the church to partner with the poor in addressing those issues and reflecting together on their common experience, thus also reflecting together on the gospel.

These, then, are the five normative presuppositions of an urban ministry which empowers. These principles are the foundation upon which all effective ministry is built. Absorb them into your very pores! For following them will radically transform your entire ministry.

# The strategy of networking

AT AN URBAN WORKSHOP at which I was speaking, one of the participants told me that I was speaking about empowerment the way an evangelist speaks about salvation. That caused me some pause. But then, as I thought about it, I found myself asking, "What is empowerment, but salvation? That's exactly what it is. 'Empowerment' and 'salvation' are really two distinct ways of talking about liberation. In the former, it is a liberation of society. And in the latter, it is a spiritual liberation."

Unfortunately, the Christian church has paid a great deal of attention to the spiritual dimensions of empowerment, but not to its societal dimensions. We Christians have often fallen into the trap of preaching a truncated and narrowed version of the gospel in which salvation deals with the interior self but not with all of life.

But the church's call is to liberation that affects all of life. It is the call to discover new life in Christ. But it is also a call to come alongside the hurting of the world and enable them to empower their lives, their slums, and their cities.

The essential strategy for empowerment is community organization. Frankly, I don't know of any other strategy to empower and liberate people that works as well. *Community organization* is that process by which the people in an urban community organize themselves to deal with the essential forces that are exploiting their community and causing them to be powerless.

The normative presuppositions presented in the previous chapter are part of that definition. The people who are best able to deal with the problem are the ones who are most affected by the problem. People excluded from participation can only be empowered by acting collectively.

Community organizing principles can also be used to strengthen and organize churches. After all, they are communities too. If a church is getting smaller and feeling defeated, these principles can be used to strengthen and encourage the people in that church community, giving them a sense of direction and purpose.

What are the principles of community organization that help us deal with groups being exploited by society around them?

### Starting with networking

The first principle of community organization is *networking*. What is networking? Networking is the intentional and systematic visiting of the people in a community by the community organizer, by pastors or by church members to identify that community's most felt issues, its most substantive problems and its pivotal leaders, to lead to that community's organizing itself to cope with its most substantive problems.

Underlying the principles of networking is the essential assumption that all human beings, however uneducated, exploited and beaten down by life, have a greater capacity to understand and act upon their situation than the most highly informed or sympathetic outsider. Every human being, no matter how deprived, is created in the image of God and as such is no less innately capable of determining his future than the most highly educated and self-determined individual.

Why network? Networking can greatly enhance the effectiveness of your church and (if you are a pastor) your credibility in the community. It can greatly inform your preaching, because you will have a strong sense of the major concerns of the people of your community—and you can bring biblical insights to those concerns. It can increase your visibility and credibility in the community. It can identify community leaders with whom it is strategic to foster relationships. It can influence church plans and programming, so that such are far more oriented toward community needs. It can identify possible prospects for later evangelization. It can create a community awareness of your church and of the congregation's concern about the community.

But these are not the primary reasons for networking. The primary purpose for networking is to provide the community organizer, pastor or church the base he or she needs to enable the empowerment of the community. No slum or squatter settlement can be organized without being networked. It is the initial means to the end of community organization.

Who networks? Well, anyone can network. Minimally, it should be the community organizers and any others working with them. But other people outside the community organizing effort could network as well. I would particularly recommend that the leaders of the church participate in the networking effort. If they have a heart for the city, they too can be drawn into the net.

How do you begin building a network? As you visit people in a given slum, call on everyone you possibly can in that neighborhood.

Visit the religious leaders of that community. Don't contact them to get them to agree with your theology. Instead call on them because they are the leaders of an organized religious community. The point is not that they believe what you do, but that they can bring people together. In Chicago, within four days, our churches could mobilize up to 2,000 people. No other institution in the city could do this. The churches had an enormous constituency.

Contact political leaders, business leaders, educational leaders and those who provide health and social services to the community. But most of all, contact the ordinary folks.

In one of the churches where I served, three to five thousand people walked by the building in a typical week. An open entrance area led into the church, with stone benches on the sides of the steps. Passersby would come by, sit on the benches, rest and chat. I would go out and casually join them. I learned so much about my community through these conversations.

Another pastor went to the bars to network. He'd sit down, have a drink, and start to talk with the people. In no time, all the people would be ringed around him, talking about the community. And they would tell him all sorts of things about the community that nobody else would share with us.

What are you seeking to discover when you network? You may think you know more about the gospel than the people in the community. You may even know more about the theoretical working of the political and social forces of that city. But *they* know more about their community. They know its joys. They know its problems. They know its history and its struggles. The first task of an urban worker, then, is to learn from the community. They are the experts and you are the novice; they are the teachers and you the student.

Pastors often ask me, "Don't people reject you when you do this?" I have never been rejected in networking visits. People are delighted that the church is coming to them asking them to tell the church about the community instead of telling them how to live their lives.

In your networking, try to learn three things.

### First, what do the people see are their issues?

Usually, a church looks at a community and asks, "What do we think are the issues of this community? Which issue should we address? What should we do to solve the problem?" The church thinks it knows better and can do better than the community. The people of the community are objects to be ministered to, and the church is the subject to do the ministry.

The result is helplessness in the community. People are taught to be recipients and beneficiaries of the church's charity. The church may feel good providing food or clothing or social services. But the people feel victimized and demeaned—and they resent the church deeply for making them feel so helpless.

Sometimes, the church tries to set up a process to encourage a sense of ownership by the community of the church's social services. But the people normally won't accept that offer of leadership, because it is not their project or even their idea. They refuse to get involved, and the burden of leadership continues upon the church. The church slowly becomes cynical about the lack of community involvement. And the community feels no ownership in the project, because the church is putting in all of the resources—not the community. So, both church and community burn out on the project.

One of the essential tasks of networking is to break this negative cycle of ministry. In networking, the goal is to learn from the community what they believe *their* needs are and how *they* choose to address those needs. And the only way to find out what the people identify as their problems and issues is to *ask* them.

### Second, who are the real leaders?

The second kind of information the networker seeks to learn from the community is who it perceives are its real leaders.

Rarely are the leaders or appointed leaders of a community its true leaders. They only perceive themselves as being the leaders. And they do exercise a kind of leadership. They exercise a negative leadership. That is, they can stop things from happening. They can block, harass, cause trouble. And this is particularly true of elected leaders. Therefore, they must have their egos stroked by being made to think they are important. If such attention is paid to them, they will not get in the way.

But there are real leaders in every community. These are the people who make a community function. These are the community's gatekeepers, caretakers, flak-catchers, and brokers. Every community has them. In fact, if a community does not have them, then it is not a community but only a random and unrelated collection of people. We will describe these leaders of a community later in this chapter.

### Third, who are the people with a "fire in their belly?"

The third piece of information the networker seeks to discover from the community is the identity of the people who really care. Again, every community has them—the people who are deeply concerned about one or more problems of the community, who care about the kids or the senior citizens or the homeless, who are really committed to the community and its issues. They may not play leadership roles in the community —in fact, often they are the work-horses—but they *care*. They have a "fire in their belly" of concern.

How do you find out these three pieces of information? It is simple. You ask the people. They will tell you.

But who is going to do the calling in the community and the asking of the people? How will they gather and store the information? Set up a calling strategy.

In one church I served, I committed one day each week to visit pivotal people in that community. My church leadership had no idea what was happening in that community. I discovered as I called that they were out of touch with that neighborhood. So, I began sharing with them what I had learned out in the community. I challenged the elders to go out and visit with me.

They hesitated, and said they'd do it if the deacons did it. So I asked the deacons, and they said they'd do it if I got the leaders of the women's association. The ladies thought it was a great idea. Eventually, we set up a calling team of 52 people, going out in teams of two or three to call.

In three months, we called on most of the pivotal and ordinary people in the community. By the end of our visiting, that congregation *knew* its community. It knew its issues and problems. It knew its history and aspirations. My people knew the real leaders of that community, not simply by reputation but face-to-face, for they had met with each leader personally. And that knowledge informed the next seven years of my ministry there (and still informs that congregation today—22 years later). It created the foundation for that church's ministry in that community, its commitment to the self-determination of that slum's poor and powerless, and the development of the interior programming and life of that congregation. I never had to argue for the necessity of that church's involvement in community organizing—no matter how confrontational or controversial the organization's actions became—simply because the congregation had identified the community's issues for itself, and in the process became committed to the people. This church had become a church of that community, working with the people on the people's issues. And their transformation had occurred solely because all the church's leadership became involved in networking.

It is essential to set up a good record-keeping system and a retrieval organization system. Obviously when you call, you will forget much of what is said. But, I discovered in my visits that if I wrote anything down during the visit, the people would conclude I was a government worker and would become cautious about any information they would share with me. Instead, I talked to people in a casual, chatty way, tried to remember what they said, and as soon as I left, wrote it down. Then I placed that information in my record-keeping system. Now, with the advent of the computer, storage and retrieval of information is made particularly efficient and easy.

**Issues and leaders**

Finding out the issues and community leaders are the most important functions of networking. What kinds of questions should be asked to reveal such information?

Start with the questions that reveal the issues. "How long have you been in this community? Is it a better community now? What was it like then? What is it like now? What bothers you about living here? What do you like about this community? What breaks your heart over this community?" Uncover the essential issues of the people. Find the roots of pride in the community. Discover if the people care intensely about their community.

Then ask questions to discover the real leaders (not the titular leaders). Find the *gatekeepers*. A community's gatekeeper is the person who decides whether or not someone "gets through the gates" (is accepted by the people) of the community. He is the official permission-giver who decides what will get done and not get done in the community. He is the "chief," the "boss," the informal leader of the community.

When you were a child in school, did you desperately want to be in a certain group in school—but no matter what you did, you couldn't get in? You ran into a gatekeeper—who for some reason didn't want you in that group! The work of the gatekeeper is a very powerful function in a neighborhood. You must identify the gate-keeper in your community.

Find the *caretakers*. I was walking through a slum in Madras. All of the children in the immediate block were playing out in the dirt in front of one of the houses. The person in that house was probably the caretaker in the neighborhood—the "Mama," the "shepherd," the one who cares, the one who listens to people when they have problems. Every community has caretakers, and they can be either men or women.

*Flak-catchers* gather the issues and the news. They gather the community's "flak." The impolite word for a flak-catcher is a "gossip." This is a tremendously important person to know. Who are the gossipers? And how can their gossip be used for the good of the community instead of being harmful?

Finally, identify the *brokers* of the community. A broker is a person who is the personal friend of a personal friend of a personal friend of a very influential person in the government or a business or multi-national corporation who can get something done for the community. The broker is the person who, because of his connections, can get a problem solved which, to be solved, needs "outside" help.

You need to ask a series of questions to identify the most pivotal person in the community—the gatekeeper. The first set of questions would be some like these: "If a group of people from this community, including you, wanted to change something here (like clean the trash from the roadway or alley or install some sewage pipes), with whom in this community would you need to talk over the idea? Who needs to agree in this neighborhood before you begin making changes?"

The second set of questions are like these: "Who can make things happen in this community? If the city government or the police or the school system is not doing right by this community, who can go to them and be listened to?" (If the person named is a governmental or elected official, ask, "Who can go to that official and get him to listen?")

The third set of questions might be as follows: "Who has moved recently into the neighborhood? How do the people of the community feel about him? Why do you think he is . . . (whatever is the evaluation of the new arrival: 'strange,' 'a loner,' 'very friendly,' etc.)? Who decided he is (. . .)?"

When the same name occurs in two or more of these sets, you may be discovering the gatekeeper. And if the same name keeps coming up in many of your interviews, you have surely identified the gatekeeper. When you discover the person who gives permission on all important community decisions, who has credibility with outside leadership, who determines who is accepted and who is rejected in the community—you have found the community's gatekeeper.

It is equally important to identify the caretaker of the community —the one who brings heart to the community, who is loved and trusted by almost all the residents. To discover him or her, a questioning scenario like this may be helpful: "If you had a major crisis at 2:00 in the morning, and none of your family was around to help, whom would you feel free to turn to for help?" When the same name keeps cropping up in interview after interview, this means you are identifying the community's caretaker.

To discover the flak-catcher, you might ask questions like these: "Suppose a neighbor down the street was letting his house go to rack-and-ruin, and you wanted him to know that people in the neighborhood did not like it—but you didn't want to confront him directly yourself. To whom would you go in this community who, if you told him of your displeasure, would inevitably carry that message to him?" If the same name keeps coming up, this is the community's flak-catcher.

To identify the broker can be a little more difficult, and usually requires a series of questions, like these: "Suppose there is a broken street light on the block, and it has been broken for months, and the city just has not come out and gotten it fixed, to whom would you go to get them to fix it?" To that question, you might get the name of the broker or of the gate-keeper. So you need to push on. "If direct contact (which is what the gate-keeper will do) does not get results, is there anybody in this community who knows someone well enough in city hall—or who knows someone who knows someone—to get results?" If that name keeps appearing in your interview, you have found the community's broker.

Why is it so important to find these four characters? These are the people necessary to have in your community organizing effort if it is going to succeed. If they are not involved with it, it will not work, no matter how much you organize. The people in the community will look to see if the most important people of the community are participating or boycotting. And on that observation, they will determine their own participation.

Think about what this means for evangelism in a community. How do you reach a neighborhood? Through mass campaigns? Door to door evangelism? Instead, build personal relationships with these four pivotal leaders. Invite them to programs of the church. Share with them what the gospel can do for them. Bring them to Christ. When you get the leading people (the gatekeeper and caretaker especially), you will not need to evangelize the community. They will become your best evangelists, because their presence in your church will encourage all the other people to come in.

The questions you ask in your networking should reveal the primary issues of the community and identify its real leadership. But there is one other piece of information you need before you have fully learned about that community from its residents. You need to find the people who have a "fire in their belly"—the people who really and deeply care about their community.

It is fairly easy to discover these people. Just pay attention to the person you are interviewing. Pay attention to the enthusiasm or boredom with which he tells you about the community. Observe whether he is excited or uninterested in the potentials of the community, whether he seems deeply concerned or is indifferent about the community's problems. If his approach seems to be nonchalant, he is most likely not a person who truly cares. But if you suspect that there is significant commitment on his part, ask him the question that will clearly reveal it: "When you look at this community (or, your neighborhood), what really makes you weep over it? What breaks your heart about this community?" Then, get him to elaborate his answer. If you are able to observe the pain, you know you have a person with a fire in his belly!

The power of networking is exhibited in the earliest stages of the organizing work World Vision is doing in the barrio Valle de los Reyes in Mexico City. The community organizer made 150 visits to 78 families in the first three months of this organizing effort. Although this was only about five percent of the total number of families in Valle de los Reyes, these calls revealed the primary issues and pivotal leaders of that barrio. Future calling uncovered additional leadership, but the seven most pivotal leaders were discovered in that initial round of calling. The primary issues never changed; additional calling only confirmed the accuracy of the initial networking.

An intriguing and unanticipated result of the networking has been the spontaneous movement of community leaders to address together issues which surfaced as a result of the networking. While continuing his networking, the organizer has worked with these spontaneous organizing activities.

A number of parents got together and organized a family development program, including childcare, adult literacy classes, family health care, non-denominational Bible education, and summertime activities for children. The people, once organized, got all six churches in the community to endorse them, and came to Vision Mundial de Mexico for funding (which they received).

Pastors indicated interest in congregational leadership development. The result was the first ecumenical lay-training program in the history of that barrio. Held in one of the churches, over 40 lay and clergy leaders gathered for two full days of Bible study, biblical social analysis and reflection on the nature of effective urban ministry addressing community issues. With World Vision's sponsorship, I came to lead the training sessions. Representatives were there from every church in the community, and three pastors who had previously had nothing to do with each other, were reconciled and began planning how they could work together for the good of Valle de los Reyes.

Networking continues in the community among pastoral leadership, gatekeepers and caretakers and the people of Valle de los Reyes. Even before the networking is completed, meetings are already being held around the primary issues identified by the community. And the empowerment of the poor and marginalized who make up Valle de los Reyes becomes increasingly a reality, as the people assume firm leadership of their emerging community.

This is networking—the first step in community organizing. Without networking, you do not have a ghost of a chance in affecting your community. You will fail in any ministry you seek to undertake there, because your work will not be based upon the people's identification of their issues and leaders. But if you network, you have done the research and relationship-building that undergirds community organizing.

## Networking in the Bible

Is networking a principle one can observe at work in the Scriptures? Most certainly. It is a pivotal ingredient in the practice of the vocation of key biblical leaders. Moses, David, Nehemiah, Jesus, Peter all reveal themselves as consummate networkers. But perhaps one of the most outstanding was Paul the Apostle.

Like Moses, Paul was a man magnificently prepared by God for the vocation to which God had called him. He was a man who thoroughly understood and was totally devoted to the Jewish faith and nation. In his own words, he testified, "I was born of the race of Israel and of the tribe of Benjamin, a Hebrew born of Hebrew parents, and I was circumcised when I was eight days old. As for the Law, I was a Pharisee; as for working for religion, I was a persecutor of the church; as far as the Law can make you perfect, I was faultless" (Phil. 3:5-6).

But, at the same time, Paul was a man who understood and appreciated the Gentiles. Born and raised in the Gentile city of Tarsus, Paul was a Roman citizen—a political lever he would use often for the sake of the church and his vocation. He understood the Greek culture, Roman law, Gentile society, pagan religions; he therefore knew profoundly the people to whom he had been called to minister. No wonder Paul could write, "I made myself a Jew to the Jews, to win the Jews . . . To those who have no Law [i.e., the Gentiles], I was free of the Law myself to win those who have no [Jewish] Law. For the weak I made myself weak. I made myself all things to all men in order to save some at any cost" (1 Cor. 9:20-22).

When Paul was converted to Christ, God sent Ananias to him with these words: "You must go [to Paul], because this man is my chosen instrument to bring my name before pagans and pagan kings and before the people of Israel" (Acts 9:15). This was exactly what Paul did. For the remainder of his life, Paul became a tireless evangelist, spreading the gospel not only throughout Judah, but primarily into the Gentile world. It was Paul's three successful missionary journeys into the pagan Roman empire which transformed Christianity from a Jewish sect into a worldwide faith for Jew and Gentile alike. A primary tool which Paul used to accomplish this task was that of networking.

Consider Paul's missionary methods, which can be gleaned rather easily from Luke's careful record in Acts. When he entered into a city, Paul did not enter alone but rather brought with him his lieutenants trained both to evangelize and to build a community of believers. His first visit in each city would be to the local synagogue, where he would proclaim the gospel; normally he met with scorn and rejection, but there were always a few Jews who listened and responded to his message.

Paul would then go to a gathering place of the Gentiles in that city (which site would likely have been previously identified by his team). He would proclaim the gospel to the Gentiles, and, most often, would again be met with scorn and rejection. But, again, there would be the few who would listen and respond.

Gathering those responsive Jews and Gentiles, Paul and his lieutenants would withdraw from public ministry in that city. They would then begin the intensive discipling of these new Christians, not only teaching them about the Christian faith but also teaching them how to develop and maintain a church (which, incidentally, was modeled upon the Jewish synagogue). As Paul and his team would work with these new converts, he would particularly encourage the Christian community to call forth each other's gifts, that each might contribute to the building of that local body of Christ (1 Cor. 12:1-14:40; Eph. 4:7, 11-13; etc.). Out of that process, the leadership of the church would be discerned and chosen, and they would receive the intense attention of Paul and his team.

Finally, it would be time for Paul and his team to leave the fledgling church. But the foundation had been built for the church to develop and grow strong. And even though the church had to make its own way in their pagan city, it was not alone, for it continued in contact with the church of Jerusalem and sister churches throughout the region. Paul and his disciples maintained a written dialogue with each of these churches and often returned for visits.

The networking modeled by St. Paul and the other pivotal leaders of Scripture is a biblical—and yet very contemporary—strategy. It is a strategy that recognizes that one must learn from the people before one can begin to minister effectively among and with the people. It is a strategy built on the reality that the only people who can effectively deal with their decaying slum are the people acting collectively who live there —and that such action cannot begin until the people identify those issues which are destroying their community. It is a particularly biblical strategy, for it affirms that God is already active in even the darkest places in a city, and has called his church to be a partner of the poor in seeking the welfare and justice of the city. Following this strategy, the church can make a difference as it lives out in the city that piece of ancient Chinese wisdom:

> *Go to the people,*
> *Live among them.*
> *Learn from them.*
> *Start with what they know.*
> *Build on what they have.*
> *But of the best of leaders,*
> *When their task is accomplished,*
> *Their work is done,*
> *The people all remark,*
> *"We have done it ourselves."*

# Coalition-building

ONCE THE NETWORKING of a slum or squatter settlement has been completed by the organizing team or churches, it is time to take the second step of community organizing. It is a very critical step, because if it is not successfully implemented, there will be no empowerment of the people. This step of coalition-building is magnificently exhibited in this statement by Nehemiah, when he discovered the walls of Jerusalem in such abysmal disrepair:

> Then I said to [the Jewish people, the priests, the authorities and the officials], "You see the trouble we are in: Jerusalem is in ruins, its gates have been burned down. Come, let us rebuild the walls of Jerusalem and suffer this indignity no longer." And I told them how the kindly favor of God had been with me, and also repeated the words the king had said to me. "Let us start!" they exclaimed, "Let us build!" (Neh. 2:17-18)

Nehemiah had networked with the leaders and ordinary people of Jerusalem. Those people had openly expressed their needs to him. Nehemiah had discovered that their deepest felt need was their sense of vulnerability to outside attack because the city's walls had been broken down.

After networking the Jews of Jerusalem, after finding our their issues and leaders and people who care, Nehemiah called them together to give voice to their issue. And he said to them, "You see the trouble *we* are in."

### The second step: coalition-building

Who is "we?" Nehemiah had been living in the lap of luxury in the Persian palace, but here he identifies himself with that exploited Jewish community by joining common cause with them. "You see the trouble *we* are in!"

In Rockford (Illinois' second largest city), I participated in the organization of a poor, black community. I was one of the few white faces the community ever saw there. One day, I was given one of the finest compliments I had ever received. "Bob, you are the blackest white person I have ever met," a community member said.

So Nehemiah identified himself with the people as he gave public voice to the issue all of them had earlier shared with him. And then Nehemiah asked them, "What are we going to do about it?"

This is the magical question of community organizing. If our aim is empowerment, we can never do something for another person. We cannot empower a child to walk by carrying him around. That child can only learn to walk by doing it. As long as the poor receive help from other people, they will never deal with their own issues.

The real task of community organizing and effective urban ministry is to empower the people to help themselves. Do nothing for them. Say with Nehemiah, "This is the problem as you have shared it with me. Now what are we going to do about it?"

The people's answer is, "Let us start! Let us build!" They are going to take charge of their own predicament. Power to the people! But then, the next question is "How do we build?" What strategy will be used?

Their first recourse is to go to the king. Oppressed, powerless people will always tend to say "Let the powerful do it—the leaders, God, the church." In Neh. 2:18, Nehemiah tells the people the king will not rebuild their walls. The king will support them, he will give them supplies, timber, bricks, stone, and mortar, but he is not going to rescue them by rebuilding their walls. They will have to do it for themselves. God may give them strength and protect them, but they have to do the work themselves.

The people declare, "Let us start! Let us build!" And so they do. They assume the responsibility of rebuilding their own walls—and their own life together in Israel.

In this regard, chapter three of Nehemiah is of particular interest. It seems to be a list of names: "Eliashib the high priest and his brother priests set about building the Sheep Gate . . . Next to them, repairs were carried out by Uzziel, a member of the goldsmiths' guild, and next to him repairs were carried out by Hananiah, of the perfumers' guild; they strengthened Jerusalem as far as the Wall of the Square" . . . and on and on the list goes.

But this is not simply a list of the Israelites working on the wall. It is Israel's plan of action. It is the strategy they devised to bring life to their declaration, "Let us build!" And what they devised, they were now carrying out—each tribe and family and person contributing with his or her own hands to the rebuilding of that portion of the wall of Jerusalem assigned to him or her.

What is of particular significance is that there is not the slightest intimation from the text that Nehemiah had anything to do with the creation of this plan of action. This was the plan that the people created for themselves, as they sought to take charge of what had become a totally unacceptable situation for them.

To organize that community, Nehemiah did three things. He led the people to identify the problem. He had them determine their own solution to the problem. He let the people undertake the implementation of their solution.

This is the most vulnerable point of any church's urban ministry. Our tendency is to come in and say, "We know best," and set up our own project. But what is the job of the community organizer at this point? Imagine that you are a part of the Smokey Valley slum in Manila and I am the community organizer. I have visited you and kept faithful records of what you have told me. Now I am ready to move to coalition building. I look at my records, and discover a fairly uniform expression of specific needs.

I go to Hector and say, "Hector, you are really concerned about your child's future and education."

He replies, "That's right."

I ask, "Do you know Sylvester?"

He says, "Yes, I do."

"Do you know that Sylvester and Mary and Judith and Juan all feel the same way as you do about their children's future?"

"No, I did not know that. I thought I was the only one."

"Why don't we all get together and talk about it?"

Maybe Hector and Sylvester go with me and tell people about a meeting at a community member's house. The people gather and we begin to talk.

Within that gathering are all kinds of strategic people—a gate-keeper or two, a caretaker, a flak-catcher and maybe a broker because I, as the community organizer, made sure they would be there. There may be a lot of people there from the community. And there are Christians and non-Christians alike—drawn together, not around common faith but a common issue.

The people begin to discuss this issue. The community organizer gets them to start talking about the problem and to analyze it. This may be a very superficial analysis. That does not matter. Some of them may say things that the community organizer disagrees with. But his opinion does not matter. The important thing is that they are discussing the deeper issues—issues of justice and oppression—by discussing their common concerns. Then the organizer asks the magical question: "What are we going to do about it?"

Together, the group begins to develop a strategy. Out of that strategy, the community finds resources. Perhaps they will come to the church or to a para-church organization and present a proposal for resources. Perhaps they will find the resources themselves. But, with these resources, the group begins to implement their strategy.

As the work goes on, the community organizer regularly talks with them about the strategy—what is going well, what is not, what they are learning about the community and about themselves. This is the process of action-reflection-action. The very nature of building a coalition is that the people act, reflect and learn from the strategy they developed to address their issue.

In the giant Mathare Valley slum of Nairobi, Kenya, World Vision's urban organizer called together the pastors, local government leaders and the valley elders with whom he had built deep levels of trust. He introduced them to the person his networking had revealed as the most pivotal and highly respected leader among that slum's poor. Zipporah Kamao was both that community's primary gatekeeper and caretaker, distributing porridge every day to 200 slum children.

Zipporah brought to this meeting her own network of community leaders. Together, grass roots and titular leaders sat down and began analyzing the issues and essential problems of Mathare Valley. Out of those meetings, a coalition was formed which created the Huruma project.

Huruma, which in Kikuyu means "Place of Compassion," is now a cooperative ministry of the people of that slum. Out of the people's identification of their own problems and the organizing of the slum's titular and grass roots leaders, a daily food distribution program, three economic development projects, and the construction of a sanitation system have evolved.

Most importantly, every church in that sector of Mathare Valley—Presbyterian, Anglican, Apostolic Faith, Pentecostal, Assemblies of God, African Inland Church, Holiness and Roman Catholic—jointly sponsor Huruma. As a result, pastors who had at one time refused to speak to each other recently united in an evangelistic crusade which presented the gospel to thousands in Mathare Valley.

What is the difference between community participation in governmental (and most churches) programs and in this kind of community empowerment? I think there is a subtle difference.

Community participation theory assumes the community must participate in planning the activity. But where does the final decision-making power actually lie? Who has the final "yes" or "no?" This is an indicator of who actually controls the project.

## Organizing and money

In community organization, the people are in control of the entire process. The people identify the issues, create the problem-solving strategy, undertake the actions and projects to implement their strategy, evaluate and determine next steps. It is their community and they decide what is best for it.

The reality, however, is that in most situations, it is the funding agency which controls the process. Even though the funding organization's rhetoric may deny it, the fact is that "he who pays the piper calls the tune." For this reason, it is strategic for a community organization that it be financially self-sufficient. Ideally, all or most of its budget should be raised from within the organization and its member churches and other community groups.

Of course, this is not always possible. In many situations, community organizations apply for grants from foundations, non-governmental organizations, denominations, church organizations and governmental agencies. But such grants should be accepted by a community organization only if it is quite clear what the conditions of funding are, and that those conditions do not deprive the community organization of any of its autonomy or action.

In Detroit, the community organization in which I was involved approached a foundation with a proposal for the funding of the coalition's strategy. The foundation leaders met, considered our proposal, and then came back to our coalition with the conditions they would set upon their funding of our strategy. Those conditions would have allowed the foundation to dictate policy to our organization.

When the group heard the stringent, paternalistic terms set by the foundation, the leader said to the president of the foundation, "You can take your $100,000 a year and shove it" (a particularly disparaging statement in U.S. culture).

That response showed who was really in control. The word spread through Detroit like wildfire—no group had ever refused a grant like that before.

In the Third World community organization, financial sufficiency is a particular problem. Most urban slum communities are so poor and their institutions (including churches) so financially strapped that adequate self-funding is an impossibility. Therefore, they are dependent on funding from outside sources (most often para-church organizations and non-government agencies, such as World Vision). It is incumbent upon the community organization not to "sell its soul for a mess of porridge," but instead to insist on its freedom to make strategic decisions on actions and projects supported by such grants. The funding agencies, in turn, need to be sensitive to their potentials of undermining the autonomy and self-determination of the community organization through their provision of funds, and do everything in their power to avoid such manipulation.

Coalition-building, then, is the second stage of community organizing. The networking has made the community organizer, the pastor, the Christians known to the community. They have come to learn from the people about the people. And if they do their networking effectively, they will discover the most deeply felt issues of the people, the real leaders of the community, and the people who really care.

The organizer then examines the results of his networking. Analyzing his records, he notes the issues which surface time and time again. He analyzes both the informal and formal power systems in that community by identifying the community's gatekeepers, caretakers, flak-catchers and brokers. He determines where the broken hearts of the community lie. Then, armed with this information, the organizer begins the building of the coalitions.

These coalitions are formed around the issues. There may be a number of coalitions the organizer encourages, each one built around a different (but deeply felt) issue of the community, or there may be just one. But as the people meet in the coalitions, they talk, they complain, they tell stories, they play "Ain't it awful!" Through such talk, what the people are actually doing is reflecting on their issue, coming to understand it better and the forces behind it which give it such power.

But the purpose of the coalition is not to gather in order to discuss. The purpose of the coalition is captured in the question that must be asked in the midst of the reflection—"What are *we* going to do about it?" The coalition sets its immediate objectives to address that issue. It creates the strategy it intends to follow to accomplish those objectives. And in that act of planning and then taking action to deal with that issue does the empowerment of the people of that slum or squatter settlement begin.

In chapter seven, we will look at the pedagogical methodology behind the organizing which enables a community to determine, implement and evaluate its strategy. In chapter eight, we will examine step-by-step the actual process for organizing a community, as it determines and carries out the strategy it sets for its own empowerment. Both the process by which the community learns and its application in carrying out organizing strategies are essential to the empowerment of the people of any marginalized or impoverished community.

# SEVEN

# The pedagogy of action
# and reflection

**Pedagogy** n. [Fr. *pedagogie*, Lt. *paedogogia*, Gr. *paidagogia*] 1.
the profession or function of a teacher; teaching 2. the art or
science of teaching; esp., instruction in teaching methods

WHAT IS IT THAT ACTUALLY EMPOWERS PEOPLE through the process of
community organization? What is the dynamic that is at work that enables
people to think that they can confront the evils in their community and
actually bring about change? What causes people to believe that they can
corporately create the future?

The dynamic that brings about this change is the process of action-
reflection-action. This process is a pedagogy, a very pivotal teaching
method which frees people from the control of old ways of thinking and
of acting, and enables them to take charge of their own future. And it is
the essential pedagogy that underlies community organizing in the coalitions and at every level of its life.

What is that pedagogy? It is simply the recognition that when
people act, their action then affects the way they think about that action.
Likewise, reflecting in a new way creates receptivity for further and more
adventurous action. Thus, action and reflection feed upon each other,
with each action leading to a deeper and more insightful reflection which,
in turn, leads to a more courageous action. Thus, a spiral is created, with
action pushing toward reflection which results in a more decisive action
which in turn causes deeper and more analytical reflection which leads
to further action, and thus to reflection. So the spiral drives deeper and
deeper.

The process at work in community organization can be dia-
grammed in the following chart:

## REFLECTION          ACTION

Felt Community
Needs

Initial Action

More Substantive
Issues

More Substantive
Projects / Advocacy
for Change

Examination of
Systems / Structures

Confrontation of
Systems / Structures

Awareness of One's
Own Complicity

Substantive,
Community-Transforming
Projects / Actions

Let us interpret the chart. As a part of building coalitions, the community organizer brings the people of the coalition together to begin reflecting on their issue. First, they think about their felt needs. For example, they might identify their felt need with the cry, "We are hungry." In the process of discussing this felt need, the organizer asks the magical question: "What are we going to do about it?"

The coalition develops a project or an action to meet this felt need. Thus, they might decide together, "Let's start a soup kitchen." So they do, purchasing food in bulk and preparing the food together to provide at least one nutritious meal each day to the community. They fund such a venture through an initial grant from a para-church organization, and sustain the soup kitchen by making a modest charge for each meal.

As the action continues, the community organizer brings the coalition together regularly to reflect on their action. What are they learning about this issue of hunger? About themselves? About the community? About those who originally opposed them?

During this early stage of reflection, a subtle change will take place in the group. Instead of thinking only of their felt need, they will begin to examine and reflect on the real issues. Thus, in our illustration, once the people's hunger begins to be assuaged as the result of the work of the soup kitchen, people will begin to ask more penetrating questions. "Why are we hungry?" they ask. "Why are we still so vulnerable?" And they answer, "We are hungry because we do not have jobs to earn money to enable us to purchase our own food."

Out of the answers coming to the coalition from this deeper level of reflection will emerge a new and more intense action. They will develop more substantive projects to address not only the felt need, but the more substantive issue. Thus, in our illustration, the coalition may decide to develop several cottage industries to supply employment for themselves and others in the community. This they do. And soon, a carpentry shop, a sewing workshop and a pottery business are successfully organized.

But reflection continues. The businesses are having a hard time entering into that city's economy. So the community organizer gets them to analyze the problem. They move into deeper reflection which examines the impersonal forces—the systems and structures of their city—which benefit by keeping some people poor and helpless. So the people conclude, "We are being denied access to the marketplace. And it is specific corporations that are shutting us out." What, then, are the people going to do about it?

The coalition now moves into an action to bring about a change in the system. This is done through the use of confrontation. For example, the people identify one corporation that they determine is pivotal to blocking the coalition. They analyze its powerful and vulnerable points and discover that it is particularly susceptible to negative public opinion. They therefore develop a campaign that will expose that corporation's actions which shut out the businesses of the poor. They confront the directors of that corporation with their intended expose and the opposition of that company, vulnerable to public opinion, crumbles. They sign legally binding documents providing access by the coalition's businesses to the marketplace.

Reflection continues as the coalition explores at ever-deepening levels the ways the political and economic establishments work for their own empowerment and the disenfranchisement of others. And the coalition takes action after action confronting the establishment to bring about a more equitable system.

Eventually the group's reflection will move into ever-greater depth, examining the political, economic, religious and social systems of the city, country and, eventually, the international area. They begin to understand that the way they have been forced to live is not because of lack of material goods or money, nor even of a few "bad" people or companies. Rather, it is primarily caused by the deeply interwoven systems of the world which exist to gain and maintain economic and political power on behalf of a few at the expense of the weak. Such growing knowledge conscientizes the group, and they begin to formulate actions which will confront the systems and structures of their city and force them into making significant changes and concessions, thus more equitably sharing power and wealth.

The process is not yet finished, however. On the final cycle, the coalition looks at their own culpability—how they themselves have contributed to the problems. At the beginning of the action-reflection-action cycle, to look at their own culpability would have been disastrous. They already felt badly about themselves, and looking at their faults would have crushed them. But at this point in the cycle of action-reflection-action, they have developed the self-esteem needed to take an honest look at themselves.

Now they are ready to talk about community-transforming actions that lead to the spiritual transformation of the community. They begin this step by identifying and confessing their own complicity in the system's exploitation of them. "We did not stand up collectively for our rights," they admit. "We allowed ourselves to be exploited." Recognition and confession of their complicity ("sinfulness") is absolutely essential if there is to be a birth of authentic community in that neighborhood. To admit to such complicity early in the process will only increase guilt and a sense of helplessness. But after it has experienced enough victories against the powers of the economic and political systems of their city, the community has developed a sense of its own capacity for self-determination. When that attitude-shift has occurred (from "victim" to "victor"), the people are then ready to look at how they have contributed to their own powerlessness. As a result of such confession, they can then take action to correct such forces within themselves and each other which contributed to their vulnerability.

Out of the action and reflection of confession of sin, the community can then move towards its own transformation. A sense of oneness with each other, the identification of and commitment to commonly developed values, and a celebration of their life together will occur. People will begin talking both publicly and privately about relationship with and thanksgiving to God—and will do so naturally and without being urged. That community will actually become "fun" to live in as people increasingly feel bonded to each other. Thus, those who began their common journey with the words, "We are hungry" conclude it by declaring, "We will increasingly advocate the values and celebrate the life of our community, so that we will remember and rejoice at who we are and will refuse to ever be exploited or marginalized again!"

A funneling process has taken place in the community. They have moved from discussing superficial problems to addressing the deep issues within themselves, bringing them to spiritual transformation. And this they have done through the pedagogy of action and reflection.

We can see that dynamic at work in the book of Nehemiah. The people thought their problem was the broken-down walls of Jerusalem. But it was not. Broken walls were a felt need, continually reminding them of their vulnerability. Building the walls was a project they could undertake. After building, they became more self-confident—self-confident enough to deal with their deeper vulnerability.

After the walls were built, Nehemiah had them reflect on their deeper problems. They realized that their issue was not just physical vulnerability, but social and spiritual vulnerability (Neh. 8:1-9:37). They reflected again on the deeper social, political, and economic forces of the Persian empire and the rulers over Palestine. They saw that they had been under one empire after another. And the reason they were poor was because they were always under an empire's rule (Neh. 9:26-37).

Next, they had to reflect on their own culpability. They recited their entire history as a people, and concluded by saying, "The trouble that we are in is because of our own unfaithfulness to God" (Neh. 9:6-17).

The entire community repented (Neh. 9:1-5). They had to realize that their own sinfulness had pulled their own community away from following God. They made the decision to undergo mass divorce from the Canaanites and separate themselves from anything that was not Jewish (Neh. 10:1-11:3; Ezra 9:1-10:17). With such an action, Israel ceased to be a state and became a people, held together by a common law given by God.

From that point on, it did not matter whether they remained together or were dispersed. "Israel" would be taken by the Jews throughout the world, no matter which cultures they were a part. Their law would give them order and meaning. The community was spiritually transformed and they became a new people (Neh. 8:1-9:5).

People reflecting and acting cause change in a community. The needs of the people cause them to take a look at their values, which moves them out to new behavior. They begin to accept those new values as being true for themselves. Subtly, their belief system begins to change. This drives them to look at the next level of needs.

When we talk about community transformation, we are talking about a conversion process in an entire community. It is most often not a sudden conversion. It is a slow, driving process causing an entire community to change their way of understanding themselves.

One of the strongest evangelistic tools in the world today has come out of the Roman Catholic Church. In Latin America, base ecclesial communities have brought profound change to the poor. Today, the church of Latin America is the church of the poor. People who originally saw themselves as poor and powerless, deserving of their poverty, are now people who take charge of their community and have the temerity to look God in the eye.

It is the task of the community organizer to lead the people in the process of reflection and action. In a profound sense, she is a teacher. He is teaching them of their dignity as human beings, of their capacity to set their own directions and to solve together their own problems, of their capability of creating the kind of community in which they want to live. The organizer is also teaching them to act collectively to mobilize their power to bring about change, and the methods they need to use to actualize these changes.

The organizer is a teacher. It is his or her task to use the pedagogy of action and reflection in all that the community organization does. He teaches in every activity. Like Jesus, the organizer does not hold formal classes, but teaches "on the run"—as events occur, as planning takes place, over cups of coffee, after the exhilaration of victory, in the midst of the mourning of defeat. And for this task of teaching through the pedagogy of action and reflection, the community organizer is rewarded with seeing a slow but steady change occurring in the people of the community.

The reward of community organizing is seeing people's lives change as they realize they don't have to remain marginalized forever. They begin to see that they are not dirt, but somebody important. When they begin to see this, that they are important to God, they are free to look at themselves and say, "I am a sinner, and I need Christ." It is exciting to see this slow, spiritual change occurring in people.

In Chicago, when my life was threatened by a prostitution ring furious with the community for closing down their business, the people of the community organization learned about the death threat. It caused them to evaluate their situation. It thrust them back into a far deeper reflection about their own lives. After all, if it could happen to me, it could happen to them.

They asked themselves, "Are we going to allow this to happen to us, or are we going to take charge of our community?" They decided to take charge. The result was concerted action against the banks.

The banks were tying to "red-line" the community, making it impossible for people to get loans or insurance to maintain their homes. This, in turn, would destroy the economic base of the community, so the people would sell their houses and land at a loss to the banks, and leave. The banks would then re-sell the property at high prices to developers. Our community organization took on the banking system of our neighborhood. And they won!

By that time, the community was unstoppable. They were on top of the world. They were then open to deal with themselves and with God.

Profound conversations began with people in the community organization. They would come to me and to other pastors and say,

"Pastor, you do not have to do this. You could have been a pastor in a quiet ministry. But you put your life on the line for us. Why?"

It was such questions that gave us permission to share about one who was willing to die for us and could transform our lives. And so the people heard, responded and received. Spiritual transformation began to take place in that community. And this so happened because we were faithful to the practice of the pedagogy of action and reflection.

# EIGHT

# Organizing for community action and projects

USING THE PEDAGOGY OF ACTION-REFLECTION-ACTION, how does a community organization usually go about the activity of organizing action and projects? After building its initial coalitions around the issues expressed by the community (chapter six), what is the process the coalition actually goes through to undertake effective action that empowers people? We will explore that process in this chapter.

### Actions and projects

When the coalitions decide what it is that they are going to *do* about an issue, they will act in one of two ways. Either they will develop a project. Or they will undertake an action. As the coalition continues its activities, it will probably develop its own admixture of projects and actions, each existing to generate power for the people through the addressing of the primary issues of that coalition.

As pointed out earlier, a project is an activity that the coalition undertakes for itself, creating and implementing what it needs to do to deal with their primary issue. Thus, in the account of Nehemiah we considered in the previous chapter, the people decided to rebuild the walls of Jerusalem themselves. That was a project.

An action is an activity undertaken by the coalition which demands of the powerbrokers (e.g., the government, economic institutions, the church) the provision of correctives or services that unit is obliged to provide by law or moral consent. Nehemiah's later confrontation of the non-Jewish governor, vice-governor and chief businessman to stop harassing the building process is an example of an action (in that case, Nehemiah armed the Jews and threatened military reprisals against the governor) (Neh. 4-5).

Actions, of course, are immediately more risky, because the coalition or community organization is taking public issue with a body which wields power in the city. And such bodies can become quite nasty when their power is threatened.

But, in a profound sense, projects long-term can often be more revolutionary. For the community to organize to change the quality of their lives in some significant way (as the Jews did in the building of the walls of Jerusalem—creating the base for much more profound change than even they recognized or bargained for) can often bring about changes which they cannot predict.

An example of an initial project occurred as the first activity of a coalition in our organizing of the slum of Nezahualcoyotl in Mexico City. Some of the women in that slum identified their primary problem as lack of work. All of them were caring for children at home. Most of them were single mothers, and had to bring their children to work. Some of them were nursing babies. All of them had a minimal education. And they didn't have any skills which they could market.

The women got together with the World Vision Mexico community organizer who asked them, "Well, what are *you* going to do about it?" What they decided to do was to form their own business—a sewing workshop. World Vision Mexico supplied the sewing machines. The ladies negotiated with a church for free space, went out and found piece-word and set up a shop.

Today, that business is so successful, it keeps eight women busy full-time. Besides paying salaries, it distributes a proportion of the profits to the ladies, maintains old and purchases new equipment, and provides a contribution to the church. The ladies have developed a training program for other women, and are developing a childcare center and Bible studies for the children.

Besides taking charge of their own lives and feeling pride in no longer being victims, these women are learning how to conduct a business, keep books, market a product, invest capital and profits, and use the banking system for the good of ordinary people.

The first activity of our community organizing effort among squatters in Madras, India were two actions. And these were followed almost immediately by a project.

When he first visited the slum, the community organizer carried a sling bag over his shoulder. If a person enters a slum carrying a sling bag, the people think he is part of the "Praise the Lord" group who come to preach and do nothing else.

It took two months for the community organizer to dispel the community's suspicions he had thoughtlessly created by not adequately researching the community. But once he did identify it, he threw out his sling bag and began building relationships with the people.

Before entering the slum, the WV India urban ministry team believed the people would choose education, health programs and jobs as needs. But the community decided instead to clean up their slum, which was filthy. City workers had neglected a legal obligation to keep the slum clean.

Slum dwellers joined forces with the community organizer and another voluntary agency's worker to meet with the city official responsible for sanitation. In doing so, they were conducting a "power analysis" (more on that later in this chapter).

At first, the official refused to see them. But then the slum community persisted with their request. Their power analysis had revealed that this official was terribly concerned about conveying an image of competence and order. When he refused to see the ten slum dwellers, they simply said they would wait to see him—and promptly sat down in the outer office and waited. The next day, they appeared with twenty people, making the same request, and when refused an interview promptly squatted. Thus it went on—the number of slum dwellers increasing each day until the office was in chaos. The official saw them.

He commissioned workers to clean up the slum and fix the electricity. And the people joined in the work, serving alongside city workers. At the end of one week, the slum was clean.

The community held a big celebration and invited the city official to join them. For the first time, the entire community discussed their neighborhood with a city official listening and participating.

The community organizer wanted to strengthen this newfound confidence. A street in the slum had no sewage system, and was filled with sludgy water. When it was mentioned as a problem, the community organizer encouraged them to address it.

Representatives from the slum collected a fixed amount of money from each house, bought a cement tube and placed it beneath the road to carry the dirty water away. They collected enough money within the slum to buy the tube without needing any money from outside sources.

Before these two changes, the community had been negative and discouraged about change in the slum. Today, they are more confident that changes can take place—and that community members can make the changes.

These two examples reveal a number of principles about community organizing. The most obvious is the difference between projects and actions. The activity of the Mexico City women to start a sewing business and the installation of the sewers in the Madras slum were projects the people chose to undertake to improve their situation. Demanding of the sanitation official to clean up the slum—a task his workers ought to have been doing all along—was an action. So was the community's insistence of a public accountability session for that official in front of that community. But in all four situations—whether project or action—what the people were doing was assuming responsibility for their own community and over their own lives by determining and taking a course of action they had devised.

A second, more subtle principle is the restoration of community. A new optimism captured both peoples. The Mexican women were learning to use the capitalist system for the people's good, rather than for a powerful few. They were, in essence, turning the tables on the economically powerful. The Madras slum dwellers became confident through their actions and project that they could really change their community and their own lives. And in fatalistically-oriented India, that is a major accomplishment.

A third factor was the role of the pedagogy of action-reflection-action. Both initial organizing activities came out of reflection. In both instances, the people sat around discussing their problems and issues with each other. The community organizer, in both instances, moved the process along. But it was the people who said, "This is what we are going to do about it!" In the India illustration, reflection occurred after the action, thrusting the group into requiring an accountability session of that official. Again, reflection led them to tackle the project of installing a sewer system. And uneducated women don't learn "how to conduct a business, keep books, market a product, invest capital and use the banking system," as did the Mexico City women, without doing a great deal of reflection.

Finally, these two stories reveal the importance of doing a power analysis (see the concluding segment of this chapter). This analysis indicated to the India slum-dwellers that the sanitation official would not be cooperative. But it also exposed his vulnerability, making the strategy develop to get his cooperation, a strategy the people knew would get results.

Whether the activity is an action or a project, however, the important factor is that the community is organizing to take charge of its present and its future. Initially, that organizing is done by each coalition. But as time goes on, each coalition discovers that they can be more effective by enabling each other to achieve their respective goals. As the organizing goes on, a primary task of the community organizer is to pull the coalitions into an umbrella organization of that community. In that organization of organizations, each coalition cooperates with the other coalitions so that more substantive goals can be reached.

### Coalitions helping coalitions

When I worked in Chicago, a bunch of little old ladies was concerned about the prostitution and pornographic trade in our community. The building directly across the street from our church was a house of ill repute.

This group of little old ladies formed a coalition against pornography in our community. They came to me and asked me, "Bob, you're a minister. What are *you* going to do about pornography and prostitution?" I told them it was not my issue; it was theirs. So what are they going to do about it? I was not going to do anything about it, but they could.

Finally, they came up with a very good scheme. It was also humorous. One maddening strategy against the powerful and a delightful strategy for the people is to get people laughing at the systems and structures. Coalitions should use humor whenever they can in their strategies. Systems and structures take themselves very seriously and hate to be laughed at.

The strategy of these little old ladies was to picket a pornographic bookstore in the most conspicuous and ridiculing way possible. To implement their strategy, these little old ladies needed a woman who was a very good speaker and the exact opposite of everyone's presuppositions about old folks. Nobody in the coalition met these requirements. But in the economic coalition, another little old lady did. The anti-pornographic coalition asked the economic coalition for the loan of the little old lady.

The group got in touch with all the television stations and newspaper reporters, informing them about an upcoming big demonstration. All the coalitions came to support the action, guaranteeing a large crowd.

Now in the United States at the time, there was a very popular and unique advertising campaign undertaken by the Burma Shave company. Knowing that as people drive on highways, they get bored, the Burma Shave company introduced a succession of small signs, each with just a few words on it—but all of the signs, considered together, conveyed a message. The aim was to tantalize people driving by to keep reading all of the signs until they got the full message.

At the same time, there was a popular song being played on the radio about little old ladies in tennis shoes from Evanston, Illinois, who were trying to get everyone to stop drinking whiskey (Evanston was the site of the Women's Christian Temperance Union).

Our little old ladies picked up on both ideas. They put on tennis shoes. They produced a bunch of placards, each with only a few words on it. And, together, they began picketing the pornographic bookstore.

These little old ladies marched back and forth in front of the store. The television stations loved the message on the placards, and situated the cameras so that each sign—held by a little old lady chanting and marching in tennis shoes—came by the camera in its turn until the whole message was broadcast all over Chicago.

The first placard said, "We might be little old ladies." The second declared, "We may be wearing tennis shoes." The third: "But we don't live in Evanston." The fourth: "We live in this community." The fifth:

"And we don't like ..." The sixth: "this bookstore, because ..." The seventh: "This store is a pornographic bookstore ..." And on and on the signs went.

And what about the little old lady borrowed from the economic coalition? The other ladies dressed her up in bluejeans and a black leather motorcycle jacket. She kept circling around the marching protestors and every so often would stick her face into a television camera and begin ranting and raving eloquently about "these dirty old men trying to corrupt us lovely young ladies with our high morals!" The reporters and television crews just loved it!

In this case, one coalition in the community not directly concerned about an issue helped another coalition to meet their goals. A joint effort made their own coalition and the whole community stronger. And in the long run, getting rid of pornography and prostitution would positively affect the value of homes and buildings in the community.

## No friends—no enemies

If a community organization becomes effective in its projects and actions, it will eventually receive external resistance. In fact, if it never receives resistance, it must question itself as to how effective it actually is.

When undertaking community organizing actions and projects, one must operate on the assumption that there are no permanent friends or enemies. The redemptive side of community organizing is the turning of an enemy into a friend by finding ways to maintain dialogue and to join in common cause.

For example, when I was community organizing in Detroit, we began with initial community-determined and implemented projects for senior citizens, youth and the many hungry people within that community. As long as our coalitions operated those programs, we had no interactions with the Detroit city government or with Detroit's mega-businesses.

But in due time, our community organization was ready to move to more substantive action. We created an advocacy program for the poor (especially with those not being accorded their rights by the Detroit city government). And our youth program began dealing with the drug issue in that community—and the police's nonchalant response to it. Soon, our standing with units of the city government began to change. They were being blocks to the people, and we were publicly exposing and harassing them. We became enemies.

As the community organization and its work continued to mature, its actions became far more substantive. The people of that community developed an ambitious housing and community redevelopment program. We undertook a major economic development project, which both trained community residents for newly-developing jobs and placed more than 300 a year in such jobs. Now our relationships with both city and the business community underwent another shift, because now we had to learn how to be partners with each other. We built networks of banks, fiduciary institutions, foundations, local and state governments, small, medium and multi-national corporations. And our approach toward each other underwent change from confrontation to cooperation. Those who were former enemies had to learn to be friends with each other for the common good.

Of course, the opposite is also true. The tragic side of community organizing is losing a friend who chooses to become an enemy. It is a sad reality that many folk join a community organization or coalition out of self-centeredness rather than a mutually-beneficial self-interest ("you scratch my back, and I'll scratch yours"). People who are in an organization purely for their own self-aggrandizement abandon it and reject you when they have accomplished their personal objectives or realize they never will; they have no further use for you, because you no longer serve their purposes. I am afraid this has happened to me many times in my work as a community organizer. And although it has now ceased to surprise me, it never ceases to hurt.

How does a community organization deal with external resistance? One important way is to maintain the right perspective. It is not your actions which are the problems. It is their entrenched self-interest. The actions and projects in which a community organization gets involved comes about because the people have been deprived of power. The poor have become the refuse heap of the economic, political, social and religious systems of the city. Those systems will always react violently to any questioning of their authority or of the hegemony they have created. Consequently, they will always try to make a community organization feel that it is their actions which are creating the problem. It is important to be aware of the systems' games, and not to fall subject to them.

### Making a power analysis

Doing a power analysis is one of the most strategic parts of community organizing. The first rule of warfare is "Know your enemy." And the community organization must know the system which it is encountering. The development of a strategy in an inner-city neighborhood in the USA will likely be significantly different from a strategy in many two-thirds world countries where legal rights may be minimal and power is both long-entrenched and without means short of revolution to remove or alter it. But in either situation, the community must learn how to analyze the power of their foes if they are going to be effective in bringing about community change.

What is a power analysis? It is the systematic and accurate study of the systems of a city as their exercise of power creates powerlessness among the people. The assumption behind a power analysis is that if there are poor or powerless people in a city, they are not there by happenstance or fate. There are exploited and oppressed people because there are people and systems that want it that way. There is only a limited amount of wealth and power and the systems seek to expropriate as much of that power as they can. This can only be done by exploiting the cheap labor of others and then keeping them weak either by oppressing them or exploiting them.

The purpose of a power analysis, therefore, is to discover and chart how power is used in the city—but to analyze it, not as a theoretical exercise, but as it will likely be used by the city's political, economic and religious systems when the community organization seeks to carry out a specific action or project. A power analysis, therefore, is not a theoretical exercise but a very concrete step in the development of any project or action.

How is a power analysis done? When the coalition or community organization has identified the primary issue which they want to address, they conduct a power analysis *before developing their strategy* to address their issue. In fact, it is the analysis that ought to provide the information the coalition or organization needs in order to be able to determine its strategy.

A power analysis has three elements to it. The first is *research*. The coalition or community organization determines the information it needs, and goes after it. Perhaps it is checking out a law to be sure what it requires of a business or a city official (think how destructive it would have been to the Madras slum group to have been informed by the government official that his office was not required by the law to clean their slum; but those slum-dwellers knew better, because they had done their research). Perhaps it is to study the title of an abandoned building or the tax records of a vacant piece of land. Perhaps it is to find out under whose authority in the government a particular problem falls. But the coalition or community organization decides what information it needs, and goes after it.

How do you gather your research? A trip to the library, or checking tax records at city hall or requesting the annual report of a corporation or studying the census data in a government office are all ways of doing the research. At first, it may be difficult to do. But as the group works at it, it will become increasingly skilled at accessing the information. And of particular help will be those people in government and the business world who will be cultivated by the community organization and, from their inside position, will become valuable sources of information. Consequently, the more you do it, the easier it will become to access information.

The second element of doing a power analysis is *interviews*. Just as the community organizer networked the community, so the people need to network governmental leaders, bureaucrats, politicians, and corporate workers associated with the action or project they want to undertake. And the only way they can do that interview is to go visit those strategically-placed individuals who can become either (temporary) friend or enemy to the community organization.

One must assume, when visiting a government official or business leader, that he is not naïve. He knows how to use power well; otherwise, he would not be where he is. But you must also recognize that he nurtures his power; despite his rhetoric, he is likely not to want to share it with anyone else. So, it is the good of the system (and of himself, as servant to the system) he prizes the most. Therefore, do not be seduced by his words of encouragement and commitment to the poor (there are some notable exceptions to the above, but they are few and far between).

So, the people intending to address their targeted issue visit the leaders and officials their research indicates will be pivotal to the success or failure of this action or project. The caller does not identify the intended activity, but simply talks with the leader as a person who is concerned about the issue. He gets from that leader the answers he needs in order to determine whether this leader will be a friend (that is, will support the action of the coalition) or an enemy (that is, will oppose the community organization on this issue).

The organization or coalition also calls on other people who know this person in order to learn more about that person—his priorities, his interests, his weaknesses, his strengths, as well as to discover whom he will listen to or not listen to.

As all this analysis is being done, the group begins the third element of a power analysis—*making a power chart*. Usually, a good-sized wall or board is needed for this purpose. As information flows in from the research and interviews, a chart is slowly constructed on that wall or board. It is a graphic description of the working relationships of people (not the official decision-making process)—who are the decision-makers and for what sort of decisions, who "blesses" those decisions but does not make them, under what circumstances roles change between decision-makers, etc. This is the actual power analysis.

I discovered in one church I pastored that three men from our official board had dinner together immediately before each meeting, decided the way each issue would go and how it would be dealt with in the board's debate. Once I discovered their strategy, I could then seek ways to make the meetings truly open and deliberative. But when I did not understand what was going on, both I and all the other members of the board were under the control of this subterfuge. And how did I discover it? By doing a power analysis of a church board whose apparently quixotic decisions stood in the way of the renewal of that congregation.

These, then, are the elements of a power analysis—research, interviewing, constructing a power chart. Knowing how power flows on the issue your group wants to address will enable the coalition to plan a strategy that will get positive results for the people.

The importance of doing a power analysis is illustrated by one confrontation of a governmental agency in Chicago. Our community had a serious problem in its public housing. That housing was being allowed by the city government to decay beyond belief. Elevators no longer worked and their shafts had become depositories of accumulated garbage and trash. The hallways were dingy, unpainted and with dimly-lit, bare lights. The buildings were infested with hoards of cockroaches and rats. But the city government was unwilling to do anything about such conditions (why they were unwilling revealed itself later on, as we discovered about the scheme of government and businesses to red-line the community, about which we wrote in the previous chapter).

We realized that the only way the people were going to get any improvement in the situation was by fighting city hall. We would have to publicly confront the director of public housing of the city. But how were we going to do that effectively? The first step was for us to quietly make a power analysis.

Among other interesting things we discovered in our power analysis was the information that the director of public housing was afraid of cockroaches and rats. That bit of information gave our community organization the clue to our confrontation of him.

The coalition planning this action met with the director and demanded he bring the housing units up to code. He refused. A month later, we returned with hundreds of protestors. They filled the rooms, the hallways, the lobby of the city hall. With such pressure, the director let our delegation in to speak with him, along with a television crew. There, after presenting our demands (which he refused to honor), we upturned on his desk boxes of live cockroaches and dead rats. He almost had a heart-attack on the spot, screaming for us to get out and (all permanently recorded on TV) finally acceding to all our demands in order to get rid of us and the plague we had brought with us. The next week, the city's clean-up crews were hard at work in each of those housing units.

Finally, a community organization must plot its strategy. Out of the power analysis, the coalition creates its strategy. It must put together a strategy based both upon its objective to empower the people and its analysis of the weak points of the system it needs to confront. That strategy will need to take advantage of the strengths of the community organization (normally, its capacity to organize large numbers of people) while confronting the system at its weakest and most vulnerable points (its credibility with the people, its need for votes, the threat of exposure of its unlawful practices). Implementation of such strategies cannot be effective if the leadership of the community organization is afraid of understanding and using power. Because power is the tool used by a few to maintain control, position and wealth. Or power is that force shared by the many that brings liberation and equitably-shared resources to all. A primary tool for using power is confrontation. Knowing how to use confrontation is pivotal, because confrontation can be one of the most effective means for bringing about change. In the next chapter we will examine the strategy of confrontation.

# NINE

# Confrontation and violence

IN THE FILM, "Cry Freedom," the South African revolutionary, Stephen Biko, was witnessing at the trial of a fellow activist. The prosecuting attorney asked, "Mr. Biko, do you advocate violence against the state?"

"No, I do not," Biko replied.

"But your writings speak a great deal about the need for confrontation," the attorney pressed.

"Yes, they do," Biko countered, "but confrontation and violence are not the same."

"How are they different, Mr. Biko?" the attorney responded, with a slight sneer.

"Well, your lordship," Steve Biko retorted, "you and I are confronting each other most directly right now, and I don't see either of us becoming violent!"

There is much confusion about the nature of confrontation and that of violence. Confrontation is simply an activity between human beings in which they are disagreeing, and because of that disagreement, are challenging one another. The word literally means "at foreheads"—that is, foreheads physically placed against one another. It is direct face-to-face encounter, seeking the end of resolution.

Violence, on the other hand, is the exercise of physical force in order to gain one's way. Whereas confrontation is verbal, violence is physical. In a profound sense, these words are not synonyms but antonyms for, by its very nature, an act of violence is the indication that confrontation has failed. Good and effective confrontation ought never to lead to violence, but should instead lead to resolution of the issue.

Confrontation is an inevitable part of effective community organizing. Violence is the prime indicator that confrontation has failed.

Christians have traditionally had trouble with confrontation. Our theology teaches us to be loving toward one another, supportive of each other, always thinking of the other rather than of one's self. Because we perceive ourselves as brother and sister to each other, we feel that confrontation is inappropriate (thus avoiding the element of confrontation which is part of the makeup of a healthy family).

Intriguingly, Christians are actually among the most confrontive people I know. (As one wag put it, "The Scripture should have said, 'Behold, how they love to fight with one another,' not 'how they love each other.'") The reason is that confrontation has gone underground. Because we believe it inappropriate to our faith, we avoid talking about it. But confrontation is inevitable in human relationships. It is actually the process that enables humans to function in relation to each other when there are pronounced differences of opinion. So when we pretend it doesn't exist among us, confrontation goes "underground;" it becomes unconscious and unspoken, and consequently much more vicious. This is why "loving" Christians are among the dirtiest fighters in the world.

If we are to enter into the empowerment of a community, and if we are to be effective in community organizing, we must learn how to confront. We must become at ease with confrontation, because no conditions will change and empowerment will not come to the city's "rag, tag and bobtail" if we do not learn how to confront.

Confrontation is found throughout the warp and woof of the Bible. The clearest example of the use of confrontation was Jesus. Our Sunday school teachers have been adept at getting us to believe in Jesus as "meek and mild." But he was hardly that. Anyone who could call his enemy "blind fools" and "brood of vipers" was not being nice. Consider these words spoken by Jesus at just one encounter:

> Alas for you, scribes and Pharisees, you hypocrites! You who pay your tithe of mint and dill and cumin [i.e., the law of paying tithes on crops even extending to herbs] and have neglected the weightier matters of the Law—justice, mercy, good faith! These you should have practiced, without neglecting the others. You blind guides! Straining out gnats and swallowing camels!

> Alas for you, scribes and Pharisees, you hypocrites! You who clean the outside of cup and dish and leave the inside full of extortion and intemperance. Blind Pharisee! Clean the inside of cup and dish first so that the outside may become clean as well.

> Alas for you, scribes and Pharisees, you hypocrites! You who are like whitewashed tombs that look handsome on the outside, but inside are full of dead men's bones and every kind of corruption. In the same way you appear to people from the outside like good honest men, but inside you are full of hypocrisy and lawlessness (Matt. 23:23-28).

It is particularly intriguing to note that Jesus used confrontation continually against the scribes, Pharisees and priests. But only once did he resort to violence—the cleansing of the Temple (Mark 11:15-19). And it could be argued that it was that act of violence which was the "final straw"—the act which pushed his adversaries, already thoroughly exasperated at him, to the final decision to have him killed. Thus, violence begets violence (of course, one could argue that this was exactly what Jesus had in mind, since his aim was to bring about his atoning crucifixion).

It is also intriguing to note that whereas Jesus was merciless toward his enemies, he was tender and loving towards the broken, rejected and marginalized of his society. A reason why this was so was because Jesus was about the task of building the church, a community of the "rag, tag and bobtail" of society. But what do I mean by "community?"

One of the best definitions of community I have heard was given by Mike Miller, director of the Organize Training Center, at a workshop he was leading. He said,

> Community is a group of people with a continuing experience, tradition and history, who support and challenge each other to act powerfully, both individually and collectively, to affirm, defend and advance their values and self-interest.

One could argue that the difference between the Jewish leaders and Jesus' community was that the leaders held to a different set of values from those of Israel's poor and powerless—a set of values that sought to preserve economic, religious and political power in the hands of a select few while exploiting those who were that society's "underclass." That was why they came under such attack from Jesus—because they would undermine and even destroy the weak and defenseless in order to strengthen their own position. When Jesus looked at the physically and spiritually poor, he saw the potential for the calling forth of a different set of values—values which would enhance relationship with God and humanity. Thus, it was among the receptive and "blessed" poor that Jesus perceived that he could best build his church.

Jesus was not the only New Testament person practicing confrontation. St. Paul was an expert at it. His letters are full of indications of confrontation of people. He not only regularly confronted the heretics and eroders of a strong church—his enemies. He even confronted his friends. Consider this statement written by Paul:

> When Peter came to Antioch, I opposed him to his face, since he was manifestly in the wrong. His custom had been to eat with the pagans [i.e., with Gentile converts who did not follow the Jewish law and were consequently considered unclean by strict Jews]. But after certain friends of James arrived he stopped doing this and kept away from them altogether for fear of the group that insisted on circumcision [i.e., subjection to the Jewish law as a

*condition for Christian salvation]. The other Jews joined him in this pretense, and even Barnabas felt himself obliged to copy their behavior.*

*When I saw they were not respecting the true meaning of the Good News, I said to Cephas in front of everyone, "In spite of being a Jew, you live like the pagans and not like the Jews, so you have no right to make the pagans copy Jewish ways" (Gal. 2:11-14).*

Nehemiah provides another clear example of the use of confrontation. In the previous chapter, we examined how Nehemiah used confrontation to resist people of power external to the Jewish community (Neh. 4:1-23). But what is particularly intriguing to note is how Nehemiah used confrontation within the Jewish community to bring about its greater maturation (Neh. 5:1-6:19).

Even as they continued in the building of the walls of Jerusalem, the Jews faced internal division. The issue is stated quite graphically in the book of Nehemiah.

*The ordinary people and their wives began complaining loudly against their brother Jews. Some said, "We are having to barter our sons and daughters to get enough corn to eat and keep us alive." Others said, "We are having to mortgage our fields, our vineyards, our houses to get corn during the famine." Still others said, "We have had to borrow money on our fields and our vineyards to pay the king's tax; and though we are of the same flesh as our brothers, and our children as good as theirs, we are having to sell our sons and our daughters into slavery; some of our daughters have even been raped! We can do nothing about it, since our fields and our vineyards are now the property of others." When I heard their complaints and these words, I was very angry (Neh. 5:1-6).*

You can take people out of the evil empire, but it is truly hard to get the empire out of people. While the Jews were rebuilding the walls of Jerusalem, the land had been subjected to a great famine. And even though the people had little enough to eat, the Persian empire still demanded their taxes. The ordinary people simply did not have enough resources to cover all their needs and obligations.

Jews who were economically strong loaned money to the less fortunate, but at exorbitant interest. Unable to pay, people had to mortgage fields, vineyards and houses, and finally had to stoop to selling their children as slaves and as sexual providers in order to meet the demands of the money-lenders.

But these were brother Jews! They were in common league in order to rebuild the walls. Their heritage was the same, and they were of one community. How could the powerful do this to the impoverished of their own people? Nehemiah was enraged at such internal injustice.

What is of particular note, however, is how Nehemiah chose to deal with such clear wrong-doing.

> *Summoning a great assembly to deal with them, I said to the authorities and officials, "To the best of our power, we have redeemed our brother Jews who had been sold to foreigners, and now you in turn are selling our brothers for us to redeem them!" They were silent and could find nothing to say. "What you are doing," I went on, "is wrong. Do you not want to walk in the fear of our God and escape the sneers of the nations, our enemies? I too, my kinsmen, and my servants have lent them money and corn. Let us cancel this debt. Return them their fields, their vineyards, their olive groves and their houses forthwith, and remit the debt on the money, corn, wine and oil which you have lent them." "We will make restitution," they replied, "we will claim nothing more from them; we will do as you say." At once I summoned the priests and made them swear to do as they had promised. Then I shook out the lap of my gown with the words, "May God do this, and shake out of his house and property any man who does not keep this promise; may he be shaken out like this and left empty!" And the whole assembly answered, "Amen," and gave praise to Yahweh. And the people kept this promise (Neh. 5:8-13).*

In this passage, we see Nehemiah directly confronting those who were profiteering from their neighbors. Earlier, he confronted them privately (Neh. 5:6-7). But getting nowhere, he then confronted them publicly (verse 8)—just as Paul confronted Peter. Nehemiah was thus using public pressure and shame to gain conformity. This is an essential strategy of effective confrontation (Gal. 6:1).

It is particularly intriguing to note how Nehemiah confronted them. He did not say, "You are bad." He said, "What you have done is wrong." In his confrontation, he separated the people from the problem.

This is an essential strategy of confrontation. Effective confrontation concentrates upon the issue at hand, not in calling the opponent names. In the community organizing I did in both Chicago and Detroit, I would seek to avoid alienating the people whom I had to confront. I would try to find ways to build relationships with them which would in essence say, "It is the issue over which we are disagreeing, but it is not that I don't like, appreciate or respect you. I affirm you; I disagree with what you are doing." Healing can occur when a person doesn't feel personally maligned. This would be of particular importance for those within the community with whom I disagreed. Although I would try to build bridges of relationship with those outside the community, I would make the building of bridges with those inside the community an absolute imperative.

Nehemiah then calls upon those whom he confronted to repent, to mend their ways, and to take major corrective steps (Neh. 5:11-13). This is also an important part of confrontation. The aim is not to crucify those with whom you disagree; it is to get changed behavior. One of the ways to accomplish this is to offer a way out—a course of action they can follow which will bring about restitution (see Neh. 5:11).

Another means for bringing about change is to publicly recognize your own culpability. Nehemiah did this (Neh. 5:14-19), as he acknowledged that he was not "holier" than those who had offended; he was as subject to the same temptation as they were, and could just as easily have yielded. After confrontation, this is a particularly important action because it recognizes your common humanity and our universal capacity to do evil.

Along with the use of confrontation, we see Nehemiah use other means to both build and to strengthen his community. Such activities are necessary components of confrontation, enabling confrontation to become healing and redemptive in nature.

Nehemiah both seeks not to profit from his community organizing and makes it clear he is not profiting. "What is more, from the day the king appointed me governor in the land of Judah, for twelve years, neither I nor my kinsmen ever ate governor's bread [i.e., drew the government's subsistence allowance, which was raised by taxes]" (Neh. 5:14). To be effective in confrontation, there must be no hint that one is receiving gain as a result of participating in the empowering of that community. To profit or even to appear to profit from organizing against the misfortune of the people compromises the entire empowering process. You must be doing it out of love for the people and love for God. Anything else is suspect.

Nehemiah also worked alongside the people. "And furthermore I worked on this wall all the time, though I owned no land; and my servants also were all employed on the work" (Neh. 5:16). The community organizer must work alongside the people in the most difficult and risky aspects of that ministry. He is not privileged, but must take the same risks and face the same dangers in confrontation as do the community leaders and everyone else in the organization. He cannot ask people to do what he is not willing to do himself. Otherwise, he lacks integrity and is perceived as a coward.

Finally, Nehemiah is very careful to define who is the enemy (Neh. 6:1-19). Confrontation is a methodology for bringing about change, a methodology which can be used on both friend and foe alike, on both those who accept the values of your community and those who are committed only to their own aggrandizement. It is therefore particularly important to differentiate between those who are truly enemies of the community (because of their commitment to an entirely different value structure) and those in the community who need reforming in order to drive the empire out of them. Therefore, to be effective in confrontation, you need to clearly identify your community's enemies and how to win against them. The real enemy must always lie outside your community, never within it.

When you confront the systems and structures of your city, there is no guarantee that violence will not occur. If you or the community organization stoops to violence, then you have lost more than that battle. You have lost the integrity of your position and the respect of your peers. But, though you completely eschew violence, you cannot guarantee that there will be no violence. The systems and structures of a city, when confronted with power and truth, can become significantly violent. The question is whether we can have enough integrity to take such violence if and when it occurs. This was the power of the civil rights movement in the United States under Martin Luther King Jr., a power which made their ultimate victory inevitable.

After the little old ladies picketed the pornographic bookstore, the community organization continued their strategy to rid our community of prostitution. We resorted to a number of confrontive strategies—taking polaroid pictures of those entering the houses of ill-repute, picketing, intimidating prominent people who were protecting this trade.

The prostitution ring was furious at our activity. And they returned confrontation with the threat of violence.

A message was put out on the informal network of our community that the prostitution ring would demonstrate to us how powerful they really were. They announced to us that one of the community's leaders would be assassinated. And the leader selected by them was me.

The community organization's leadership met to decide what to do. We realized that we could not yield to this intimidation and maintain our credibility and effectiveness as an organization. To yield to this threat would be for us to surrender to all the powers of darkness (both human and spiritual) in that community. The people would never stand up to intimidation and exploitation again. Our community would be doomed.

We decided we would not be intimidated. We would continue our attack upon the prostitution trade. And we—and I—would take our chances.

For the next twelve months, as I stepped into the pulpit of my church each Sunday, I did not know if I would live to finish that Sunday's sermon. As I would climb into my car, I never knew whether this would be the time that, upon the turn of my key in the ignition, my automobile would blow up. As I walked the streets of my community to visit with its people, I never knew if I might get gunned down from a speeding car. Every minute of every day for twelve long months, I—and the entire leadership of that community organization—lived in terror of my death.

But we would not be intimidated. We continued our war against the prostitution and criminal forces of that community.

Those twelve months were hell for me. The spiritual warfare I went through is almost impossible to describe. To simply go through the tasks of each day—never mind battling the primary issues of our poor neighborhood—became an almost insurmountable obstacle for me. It brought me up against myself and my personal lack of spiritual resources. And that was the beginning of my own struggle to develop the spiritual base I needed in order to sustain myself in the warfare with my city's principalities and powers (but that's another story).

No attempt was ever made against my life. We do not know whether they ever intended to carry out the threat. We don't know whether they discovered we couldn't be scared away. We don't know whether they decided that carrying out the threat wasn't worth it. All we know is that about ten months later, the pimps and prostitutes and crime lords began moving out. And by the end of the year, they were all gone. And all because we would not be intimidated.

Confrontation—this is a primary means for bringing about the empowerment of the poor of a community. Such empowerment cannot happen without the use of confrontation. Therefore, as those who seek the empowerment of people and as Christians, we should not avoid the use of it. To choose not to confront is to guarantee that you will surrender your community to all the powers of human, systemic and spiritual darkness arrayed against the poor and the people of God. Refusal to use it will guarantee that the people will never stand up to intimidation and exploitation again. And your community will be doomed.

# TEN

# Leadership development
# in the community

LEADERSHIP DEVELOPMENT IS ESSENTIAL to community organizing. A community organization is only as good as its leaders. Saul Alinsky, the father of community organization, used to say that a community organizer is always an insult to the community. What he meant by that is that a community organizer is always a reminder that the community needed outside intervention to become empowered. Consequently, as a community organizer, your aim must be to work yourself out of a job. The way to do this is through leadership development. Your primary task is to discern the people in the community who have leadership potential, train them, and call them forth, so that someday the organization can get along without you.

Where do you find potential leaders? Look among the natural leaders of the community—the gatekeepers, flak-catchers, caretakers, and brokers. Look among the people with fire in their bellies—those whom you earlier identified in your networking as those who really care. Look among those who play a leadership role in the community because of their position—pastors, teachers, respected business people. And look among the ordinary people, the quiet people. One of the best leaders I ever nurtured was a mother and grandmother in Detroit whose entire identification with that neighborhood had earlier been as a housewife and homemaker.

For what roles are you developing these leaders? You are preparing some of them to lead the community. They will be the spokespeople, the ones up front who, because of their charisma, style and articulate nature are the ones best equipped to speak for the organization.

Others will be the visionaries, the ones who naturally set directions, who can dream dreams, create crazy ideas, set long-range objectives. Still others will be the mobilizers, the ones who can both plan for and organize for specific action.

All are needed to make a community self-determined. And, often, the natural skills of gatekeepers, caretakers, flak-catchers and brokers enable them to hone their skills and grow rapidly into accomplished leaders of the community.

An organizer needs to discover those who have the capability of leading the community organization. Often, the spokespeople, visionaries and mobilizers can assume this responsibility. But not necessarily. Sometimes, there are the quiet people who can be the true administrators and organizers who make a community organization truly function. Those people you need to find.

How do you go about training leaders? Not by setting up courses or leadership institutes, unless the people are already accustomed to attending courses. Find ways of training them based on how they already go about learning. The action-reflection-action process of coalitions is one of the best ways to nurture and train the people. That style of leadership development is closer to Jesus' style of discipling than is a professor in the classroom. It is walking the roads of Galilee and using the circumstances around you to teach.

The community organizer who trained me never said to me, "Linthicum, I see you have potential to be a community organizer. Let me train you." It was only years later that I realized what he had done. He took me everywhere, asking me what was going on. We'd go through an experience and then he'd ask me to join him over coffee. He'd ask me questions, like: "Bob, why did the official say what he did?"

When it came to confronting someone, that organizer would lead us through a role-play. We'd take different parts—the mayor, the officials, the crowd. And I would have to pretend to go into the government official's office and convince him to do something. Then we'd discuss it. And do it all over again. I never opened a textbook. What he did was teach me right in that situation. This is how to prepare someone for leadership in the community.

One of the most unusual ways of doing leadership development I have heard about was in a Madras slum World Vision was organizing. Most of the people living in that slum, because of their religion, believe that the quality of their former lives determines their present condition and their caste. They accept their poverty as inevitable, enduring it in order to be reincarnated into a better situation and caste. Because the people of that slum were of the lowest caste, they concluded they were worthless and deserving of their humiliating place in society. How would the community organizer get the people to begin perceiving themselves in a new way which could lead to their external—and internal—liberation?

Selecting several youth who were not held captive by this perception of humanity, the organizer got them to wrestle with this issue. The youth decided to create a street drama which would graphically show the slum-dwellers that they could do something to change the situation.

This they did. The youth presented their street play, not once but over and over again on the streets of that slum. People came swarming to be entertained. And instead, they learned about themselves and their community and what they could do. Following each presentation of the play, the youth would engage the gathered people in discussion about the play. As they talked, the people realized that their greatest oppressor was themselves—that their values prevented them from taking action to help either themselves or each other.

Community women, motivated by the drama, decided to make baskets for a living. They turned to World Vision for assistance. But World Vision was careful not to offer financial help. Instead the organizer helped the women figure out what they could do to develop their own business.

Each woman contributed ten rupees a month to pay for their teacher and supplies. They began to learn how to make and market baskets. Because of their investment, they took their lessons seriously and soon began to sell the baskets they made.

Thus, the community organizer engaged two groups of people in leadership development. By motivating the youth to create and present the play, he enabled them to reflect on their own limitations created by their values. And such reflection was deep enough that the youth were able to lead in discussion small groups of the slum community gathered for the street-drama.

The community organizer motivated some women toward income-generating activities as a result of the street-drama. From both of these groups, leaders began to emerge, and the organizer trained, nurtured and developed them.

It is easy for an organizer to become caught up in the issues and excitement of organizing the community and ignore the more painstaking and difficult task of perceiving, calling forth and training leaders. But the success of the entire organizing venture rests on the ability of the organizer to reproduce himself in the people he prepares for leadership. As the Apostle Paul wrote for Timothy: "You have heard everything that I teach; [now] hand it on to reliable people so that they in turn will be able to teach others" (2 Tim. 2:2).

In one of the courses I teach on community organizing, I use the story of Nehemiah as a prime example of how to do organizing. Invariably I get asked by the students, "Did Nehemiah do *everything* perfectly?" The answer, of course, is that he did not. He did not train adequate leadership to follow him. And the result of that failure was the near collapse of that organizing effort, and of the aborting of a fetal Judaism. The book of Nehemiah does not tell us that the great organizer failed to produce leaders. But the evidences of Nehemiah's failure clearly witness to that fact in the book's concluding chapter.

Chapter 13 reports that, once completing the reorganization of the life of Israel, Nehemiah returned to the court of Artaxerxes, monarch of the Persian empire. But word soon reached him that Jerusalem was in a state of collapse, the noble experiment clearly failing.

Nehemiah returned, not only to chaos, but to gross malfeasance of office. The leaders he had left in charge of the nation and temple were not only involved in misrule but in massive embezzlement of funds. The ruling priestly caste—the Levites—were neither obeying the law of Moses nor leading the people in the worship of God. The people were conducting business on the Sabbath as they would on any other day, had married heathen women and were freely disobeying all the covenants they had so enthusiastically embraced earlier. The entire effort to reorganize Israel and to secure the future of Judaism had come unglued.

Nehemiah went quickly to work. He removed both the high priest and the governor from office, severely reprimanded the Levites and priests, and restored the strict observance of the Sabbath. "And so I purged them of everything foreign; I drew up regulations for the priests and Levites defining each man's duty, and regulations for the deliveries of wood at stated times, and for the first-fruits," (Neh. 13:30-31) Nehemiah wrote.

Recognizing the error he had made, Nehemiah created far more precise and stringent regulations for the ordering of Israel's life, selected a new leadership and diligently trained them to provide firm direction to the people of Israel. Only after he adequately trained leadership was the chastened Nehemiah free to once more return to Persia, now leaving the country in the hands of men and women who would remain faithful to the covenants the nation had made with God.

The community organizer must continually be looking for people to train, and then train them right in the field, right on the job. This requires a great deal of discipline. You have to keep your eyes open for potential leaders. You have to build personal relationships. You have to build trust in those relationships. You have to design a training program appropriate to the way a person learns. And you must be determined to prepare a new generation of leadership.

The success of all you do in community organizing depends on how well you train leaders to take over after you leave. Eventually, you *will* leave. You can insult the community with your presence for only so long.

When you leave, if you leave that community with leadership unprepared (as did Nehemiah), the organizing effort will collapse—no matter how brilliantly it was organized. But if you "impart to reliable people" what you have learned, the organization will remain the voice and hope of the people for decades to come.

In Chicago, the Organization of the North East began with a small group of us working with the community organizer. He trained and led us through the organizing process, and under this tutelage, we became the first generation of leadership in that organization. The years were 1972 through 1975.

In 1975, I left that organization to take a pastorate in the Detroit area; the community organizer also left, his organizing task completed. By 1978, every leader who had been a part of that initial small group that the organizer had trained was gone. But every one of us had trained at least one person to take our place. Those people became the new leaders of that community organization.

Within four or five years, that second generation of leadership had left that city. But faithful to the task, that generation had in turn trained new leaders. That third generation eventually reproduced itself once again, preparing a fourth generation of leaders. That fourth generation are the people running that organization today.

On a recent visit I made to Chicago, a friend told me that the Organization of the North East is a most effective voice for the poor in Chicago. There is only one reason for this. We paid attention to leadership development throughout the organization's history. We passed on what we knew to reliable men and women who, in turn, passed it on to others. Without leadership development, everything you have done will pass away. But with it, the future is constantly being created anew for the people of your community.

# ELEVEN

# Towards community

THE PURPOSE OF COMMUNITY ORGANIZATION is to provide the powerless poor with the vehicle that will enable them to change their own situation. And the way the poor can act powerfully is to act collectively.

We have explored primary strategies which lead to the empowerment of the poor. Such strategies include the community organizer's self-identification with the poor, networking the community to identify the community's primary issues, leadership and those who care, building coalitions which become involved in actions carrying out strategies created by the coalition to confront those issues. We have examined tools the people use to carry out successful action—research and power analyses, undertaking projects and actions, creating a continuing rhythm of reflection and action, using both confrontation and humor as appropriate tactics, identifying and training grass-roots leadership. All these are strategies and tactics that are at the disposal of organizer and community alike to empower the poor and exploited.

## Organizing for empowerment

But the process of community organization does not end with the effective use of people-based coalitions to address their primary issues. Such activity, while empowering, will not continue to liberate the marginalized and oppressed because it has not yet created a permanent organization that will go on representing the interests of the people no matter how the issues might change. The next step of community organizing is needed to provide that permanent means to represent the interests of that formerly defenseless community.

### *From coalitions to community organization*

The next step is to weld the coalitions into a permanent organization of the community. This organization should be the community's organization—that organization (and likely the community's only-such organization) that represents all the interests and groups in that community. Every other community group represents the self-interest of that particular group. Each church, for example, while committed to the work of Christ's body throughout the world, primarily concentrates on building up its own body-life and institution. A political party is committed to its dominance of the politics of that community, including the defeat of any other party that might threaten such dominance. The schools are interested exclusively in education, the Rose Growers Society in raising prize roses, the business association in improving business. Even government, which feigns a commitment to equal treatment of all groups before the law is, in reality, most interested in sustaining its own power. No group has the full interest of the entire community at heart. That is what contributes to the powerlessness of any poor community.

Coalitions provide the means by which the people of the community can mobilize around commonly identified issues and carry out actions together which can modify or even radically alter those issues. This is extremely empowering, especially for people who, before the creation of the coalitions, felt they were vulnerable victims in front of those issues. But while coalitions will provide for immediate empowerment, they will not sustain the empowerment of a people. Only the creation of a permanent organization can do that. Such an organization of the community can be created in this way.

In chapter six, I introduced the idea of coalitions supporting each other in the accomplishment of their respective objectives. This is the discovery of an enlightened self-interest—that my interests are more significantly met by supporting another coalition in the achievement of their interests (while expecting the same from them) than by exclusively concentrating on my own concerns.

As the community organizer calls the various coalitions into being, he lets them know about each other. Soon after each coalition begins to experience success and some level of stability, he begins to call their leaders together. The coalition leaders begin meeting regularly to explore common interests, to keep each other informed and to encourage each other. It is then only a matter of time before they begin to support each other's efforts, as the economic coalition did for the coalition fighting prostitution in the example I presented in chapter seven.

When the leadership of the coalitions begin to experience how much they need each other to accomplish their respective objectives, the community organizer can move them into the next state of mobilization. They can create a permanent organization with elected leadership, with the coalitions as action groups of that organization. They can begin holding official meetings of the organization, plan actions together, set and raise budget and plan comprehensive strategy together.

### Hearings

Particularly important at this stage is the holding of public hearings. The membership of all the coalitions would be expected to attend these occasional events (thus guaranteeing a good attendance), and invitations would be extended to the entire community, but particularly to the leaders of the various groups and institutions in the community. The organization would take special pains to get those leaders there through personal invitations, follow-up phone calls, and even sending an escort to pick them up and bring them to the hearings.

The hearings are strategic to the creation of a community awareness of and respect for this budding organization. Along with winning actions that empower the community, these hearings create credibility for the organization. Each hearing can be developed by a coalition, and exists to make public the issue, to build people's anger over that issue, and to organize for action. Of particular importance are those hearings which are accountability sessions, when governmental or business leaders who are present at the meeting are held accountable for their decisions, actions or lack of action on the issue. It was an accountability session to which the people of that Madras slum called the sanitation director (chapter eight) when they celebrated the cleaning up of their slum by the city workers.

A later step can be that of declaring the permanent organization the community's organization, and taking the necessary steps to make it a legally incorporated body in that nation, state or city. It is at this time that the organizations of the community—its churches, clubs, fraternal organizations, unions, and other groups—are recruited for membership. In this way, the community organization becomes an organization of organizations—the organization which pulls together, not only the people and the coalitions of that community, but all its organizations, as well, for common action.

It is also important, at this stage, that the organization should be financially independent. All the operating costs of the community organization should be raised from the community itself, primarily through the fees paid by the organizations and people who join the organization. Earlier in this book, I pointed out that this objective is particularly hard for community organizations in the two-thirds world to achieve. But even if that is true, it should be the ideal toward which they are working. Any organization funded from outside the community is terribly vulnerable, because the continuance of the organization depends upon the continuance of that funding source. And that makes the community organization vulnerable and potentially disempowered.

By this stage in its development, the community organization legally exists. But just because it *legally* exists does not mean it *officially* exists. It is not yet recognized as the sole and authoritative voice for the community. How does it make that transition? It does so through the holding of a community congress.

### The community congress

The community congress is the final step in the creation of a community organization. A congress is different from a convention. A convention is a body of people temporarily drawn together to meet around a common theme and agenda. A congress, on the other hand, is an official gathering of an organization representing its constituent parts, with each participant a legal delegate of his sponsoring organization and commissioned as such to vote on behalf of his organization in the decisions the congress makes.

The purpose of the community congress is to set the priorities and directions of the community and to position the emerging community organization as the officially-sanctioned body to mobilize the community to meet those priorities and directions. In that congress, each dues-paying organization (churches, community groups, clubs, fraternal organizations, unions, political parties) is seated, with its officially designated delegates and alternates. If the community organization has personal memberships as well, a prior meeting of those holding individual memberships is held to select their delegates, as well (in essence, the individual members become an "organization" at the congress). At the congress, each coalition presents a report on the addressing of its issue through its actions and projects. Speeches are made. Songs are sung. And then, a platform committee presents recommended objectives, positions and actions for the community to undertake for the next year. Some of these objectives and strategies have come out of the work of the coalition over the previous year. And some will come out of the community organization's anticipation of emerging issues for the new year. The congress then debates the platform committee's recommendations and votes, establishing the objectives of the community for the next year and mutually acknowledging the community organization as the body responsible for leading that community into the accomplishment of those goals. Celebration breaks out following that action, and the congress comes to a close. The community organization is now clearly acknowledged by the people and organizations of that community as its leader, and empowerment has now been given an official recognition and permanence it did not have in the coalitions.

Of course, a congress like this does not just *happen*! It takes nine months to a year of preparation. And it takes a great deal of the energy of that budding community organization. Not only does a platform committee have the painstaking task of creating the community's objectives for the next year (which means public hearings, as well as countless meetings with the coalitions and the leaders of pivotal groups in the community). An arrangements committee must handle the multitudinous details of an event of this magnitude, not least of which is selection of the venue. A delegate committee must recruit all participating organizations, obtain from them and create delegate and alternate lists, and establish the delegate-selection process for individual members. A program committee must create and execute the entire program. A celebration committee must plan the all-important acts of celebration, which create a sense of unity and identification with each other. The coalitions must create intriguing presentations. And on and on it goes. So it is a major task of community mobilization. But it is worth it in creating an original and single-minded community with permanent empowerment through its community organization.

The congress is the type of vehicle which would likely prove most effective in countries with strong democratic traditions. What would be used in more autocratic countries would have to be contextualized to their own situations. But there would need to be a significant activity that would catalyze the community organization comparable to what the community congress does in a democratically oriented country.

Creating and bringing to fruition the Community Congress of the Organization of the North East was the capstone of my involvement in community organizing in Chicago. It came at the close of three years of intense community organizing among the 120,000 people of the Edgewater-Uptown communities of Chicago. It took nine months of preparation to achieve it. But that congress set the priorities and directions of that community which can still be felt fifteen years after it was held.

I was one of a team of eight people who planned and managed the implementation of the congress. One month before the congress was to be held, I was called to serve another church in the Detroit area, some 300 miles from Chicago. Two weeks before the congress was to be held, I left for my new church.

But I could not stay away. I had to return to be at that congress. Because I was no longer pastor of the church I had served in Chicago (which was one of the organizations seated at the congress), I could not be a delegate. But I was allowed to be an observer.

The congress began, with more than 5,000 delegates assembled in that hall. Placards announced where each delegation was sitting. The entrance hall held displays of the work of the coalitions. The stage was gaily decorated in red, white and blue (the colors of the flag of the U.S.A.).

The congress began. For the next three hours, as I stood at the back of the mammoth hall, I watched the congress unfold. The reports of the various coalitions brought tears to my eyes as I remembered actions in which I participated, picket lines and confrontations, laughter and crazy ideas, fears and a death threat. And then the committee I had chaired— the platform committee—made its report, its vice-chair taking my place. The objectives and priorities of that giant community were set for the next year. And suddenly, the room was full of celebration—band-playing, balloons falling from the ceiling, people hugging and clapping and dancing and standing on chairs. This community of 120,000 souls, abandoned by the city council, exploited by business opportunists, "messed over" by the city's political and economic systems for a generation, had now declared that it was somebody. It now had a powerful future, because its people had taken charge of that future!

It was now time to leave. I no longer belonged in that community or its celebration. I quietly slipped out of the hall and into the foyer, the noise of a rejoicing people growing dimmer behind me.

Suddenly a door opened on the other side of the foyer, and the community organizer of the Organization of the North East—the man who had not only taught me so much about community organization those past three years but who had also become a brother to me in a common commitment to the empowerment of the weak—came through the door. We met at the center of the foyer and silently walked outside the building and down the steps.

We reached the bottom step. He turned to me and said, "Goodbye Bob." "Goodbye...and thanks!" I replied. We embraced, turned and walked off in opposite directions down the street. With the completion of the congress, our work in Chicago was over. Now, we went our separate ways—he to begin organizing another community in Tennessee. And I? I was off to Detroit to engage both the poor and the powerful in a ministry built upon the things that man had taught me. One community was now empowered. It was time to begin the empowerment of two others.

### The building of a community

Of course, simply holding a community congress at the close of a three-year organizing drive is not the completion of community organizing. But it is the completion of the *creation* of an organization designed to provide a permanent means for the empowerment of the people and institutions of a community—no matter how many generations lead it. The making of a community begins with the successful creation of a community organization. But the process of empowerment must continue on from there. What does such continuation look like?

The final purpose of community organization is not simply to enable the weak and vulnerable to confront the issues which are destroying them. It is not to enable a community to act powerfully by acting corporately. The primary purpose of a community organization is to *create a community*—to create out of a victimized, marginalized, destructive neighborhood a community whose quality of life is such that people find fulfillment and joy in living there. If such a community is not created, then all that one has accomplished through community organizing is the replacement of one oppressor by another in the tyranny of the now-powerful poor. The power of the oppressor must be replaced by a quality of corporate life which is of such superiority to either that of the formerly oppressed or of their oppressors that it brings purpose, direction, joy and fulfillment to all who experience it. That is the true objective of community organization.

Earlier, I quoted Mike Miller's definition of community. He wrote, "Community is a group of people with a continuing experience, tradition and history, who support and challenge each other to act powerfully, both individually and collectively, to affirm, defend and advance their values and self-interest" (chapter nine). How is such community created? And what does community organization contribute to the creation of a people who are committed to each other and their tradition? How is a defeated people spiritually transformed through Christian-based community organizing?

No significant transformation can occur if the cultural heritage of the people is ignored. People must either revise and integrate old customs with new ideas or abandon them altogether and seek new customs. People can make great sacrifices for the good of the community if they see that their action will affirm their cultural heritage.

In the United States, former slaves began to say "Black is beautiful," after tracing their roots back to Africa and their cultural heritage there. They began to see that they were not the sons and daughters simply of slaves, but of kings and queens of great African civilizations. They discovered a heritage in the past that strengthened them to do the work of liberation they had to do in the present.

Celebrating culture is most meaningful when it centers on worshipping God. In Nehemiah, the problem was not the walls of Jerusalem. The problem was far deeper. Building the walls only met a felt need of the people. But in Neh. 8:3, the people gathered as one man, asking Ezra to bring the Law and read it to them. They began reciting the book of the Law, recognizing who they were by looking at their spiritual heritage. What did it mean to be an Israelite? Should they cower before the Canaanites? Not at all. They were a people with a thousand-year heritage who had come out of slavery to build a life for themselves in a ravaged promised land.

Worship by the people demonstrates to the people their depths, showing them their greater potential. Worship is the advantage church-based community organization affords. But the same spirit of worship can be used in a secular organization to celebrate cultural heritages.

In chapter nine of Nehemiah, the celebration began. The Jews recited their history in terms of the great things God had done for them.

"God delivered us from Pharaoh; God can deliver us from Sanballat," they, in essence, declared.

But celebration of the past is not enough. A part of the whole process of celebration is "rubbing raw some of the discontent of the people." Saul Alinsky said it must be like rubbing a raw sore on your skin —massaging the sore spot in people's lives, so they get uncomfortable enough to act.

In Nehemiah, the people became more and more aroused over their unjust situation. This is necessary for the emerging spirituality of a people. It is not enough to celebrate who they once were. They have to say, "Woe is me, for I am one with unclean lips." Without a divine discontent in people, they will never be open to change. It is not enough to say, "It was the fault of those other guys." They have to see they have contributed to their own discontent.

We see that dynamic at work with the people of Israel. In verse 37 of Nehemiah 9, the people tell God that he has been just, while they have been wicked.

Community transformation requires deep reflection, centered around an act of worship that celebrates the people's heritage, and a recognition that they have helped create their discontent. But the community needs to take even more intense action for transformation to become complete. This is the community-reformulating phase of community organization. The community studies how to re-structure their lives to become truly liberated. Nehemiah used participatory democracy to do this. The people came up with the plan of action.

At this stage, the community should create a symbolic means of sharing their commitment to each other. Christians use baptism to do this —a sign to make clear the commitment. Jews do it through circumcision. In Nehemiah 9:38, the people made a firm agreement in writing. They had a signing ceremony, saying this is who we are, this is what we are committing ourselves to. Resolve then comes to do what needs to be done.

Their first resolution magnificently demonstrated their commitment—"We will now rebuild the temple." They integrated their resolution into their lives. Again, they used a symbol to evoke a sense of identity as a community—the temple, a symbol from their past. They had recognized the real problem was the sustaining of Israel. Were they willing to give up their own prerogatives to create a new community? They reinstituted the acts of worship from the past that bound them together as a people (Neh. 10:32-39).

The next crucial step, which up to that point had seemed the most difficult step of all, was to repopulate the city of Jerusalem. To do this, they used yet another symbol—the symbol of the tithe, the heart of Mosaic Judaism. One-tenth of all of Israel would have to give up their heritage in the countryside to move into the city and live there for the rest of their lives (Neh. 11:1-3).

The leaders all came to settle in Jerusalem. Israelite leaders did not ask the people to do anything they would not do themselves. The rest of the people drew lots. From the law, they read that God would bless if God's people gave the minimum of one-tenth. So they decided to tithe the people. The community committed itself to select one-tenth of the families and people so that they left their homes and villages, and repopulated the city of Jerusalem.

People began to make the hard decisions essential to the life of the community. The hardest decision of all came at the end. But I suspect that way back in the beginning, fifteen years earlier in Susa, Nehemiah knew this is what it would take to rebuild Jerusalem. The hardest thing to do was the decision of mass divorce (Neh. 10:30; Ezra 10:1-17).

Every Jew who was married to a Canaanite woman and every Jewess married to a Canaanite man divorced. In one sense, this was an act of injustice. But in a more crucial sense, it was an absolutely essential act for the survival of the community.

For their hard decision, you will not find Nehemiah playing any kind of leadership role. The people had accepted the responsibility to make these hard decisions. They placed upon themselves things that Nehemiah could not have placed upon them.

My wife is a kindergarten teacher. When a child is naughty, she asks the class to decide what punishment to give him. It is always a more severe punishment than she would ever give. And all of them want to avoid this judgment by their peers and so they are good. In Nehemiah, the people set stricter requirements on themselves than anyone else could.

Thus it is that, in chapter 12, we witness the rebirth of the Jewish community. They celebrate their victories and that new birth.

Do not think that Christianity exists because of Israel. It exists because of what Nehemiah and Ezra did in organizing the community. They closed the door on the period of Israelite history dominated by the state of Israel and opened the door on the religion of Judaism. It was the religion of Judaism that preserved the Israelite people, not the state. The Torah preserved Israel, even through the dispersion. The place called Israel, where Jesus was born, existed because of what Ezra and Nehemiah did. Moses was the father of Israel. Nehemiah was the father of the Jews.

The story of Nehemiah ends with one of the most beautiful passages in Scripture. Nehemiah finishes his story of the transformation of Israel with these words: "Remember me, my God, for my happiness" (Neh. 13:3).

What had happened to Nehemiah? He was financially destroyed, he had given up fifteen years of his career, destroying himself economically and politically. What, then, was his happiness?

He had set a people free. He had liberated a people. He had not only organized them to rebuild walls but to rebuild their life together, to become a new and purposeful people. An entire people had been transformed holistically. And that is the happiness of community organizing.

*TWELVE*

---

# The church and community organization

WE ARE NOW APPROACHING the end of our reflection together. But before it is complete, it is important that we consider the unique relationship between community organization and the church. Why should the church be involved in community organization? Why, of all institutions, should a body that names its Lord as "the Prince of Peace," fully participate in an organization that confronts, resists the authorities, empowers the poor and generally makes trouble? We will conclude our study together by considering the reasons why the church should be a committed participant in the community's organization.

**God demands it**

There is, of course, no Scripture which says, "Thou shalt be involved in community organization!" But the themes of justice and of commitment to the empowering of the poor dominate the Scripture. Shaping the entire biblical message is a profound social analysis that evangelicals miss because we interpret passages making a social statement from an individualistic perspective.

For example, we miss the power of a primary command such as: "Listen, Israel: Yahweh our God is the one Yahweh. You shall love Yahweh your God with all your heart, with all your soul, with all your strength..." (Deut. 6:4-5)

Because of our bias toward the salvation of individuals, evangelicals automatically interpret this passage individualistically whenever we read it. But look at that statement. It is not a commandment given to Israelites, but to Israel. It is a corporate statement, a social statement—calling the nation to love God with every fiber of its being.

The Scriptures present nations, cities, businesses, churches, and even families as bodies that are made up of these interlocking systems—a religious system (that is, that structure by which that social institution moves into relationship with God), a political system (that structure which orders the life of that community) and an economic system (that structure which provides the material support of the nation, city, business, church or family). As we pointed out in chapter one, these systems have been created by God to make of our corporate bodies a paradise for humanity and, consequently, to bring glory to God.

The religious system has been created by God to bring the nation, city, religious institution or family into relationship with God. For this is why corporate life—as well as individual—was created: so that humanity might glorify God and enjoy God forever. The political system was created by God to bring a Godly order to the institution—an order based upon equitable justice for all as the inevitable outworking of a corporate deepening of relationship with God. Finally, the economic system was created by God to steward responsively the resources of the nation, city, business, church or family. God was perceived as the owner of everything and the people as God's trustees, caring for God's wealth by using that wealth to maintain economic equality and justice for all citizens.

Of course, we know society does not fit that description. Greed, avarice, the lust for power, the need for prestige seem to dominate all individual and corporate human relationships. And the Bible is not shy about analyzing what went wrong. Whether describing the confrontation between Moses and Pharaoh, the gradual corruption of Israel's kings, the misuse of power by Nebuchadnezzer in Babylon, the coterie of priests who put Jesus to death or the systems of Satan and God as represented in the whore Babylon (Rev. 17-18) and the New Jerusalem (Rev. 20-21), the Bible analyzes the gradual corruption of the system God has created.

That corruption begins with money. The economic leaders determine that they are not stewards but owners of an institution's wealth. Eventually they will not only seek honest gain but will cheat in business, charge unfair interest and find legal ways to steal from the people — thus exploiting an increasingly vulnerable people to build their own estates (Ezek. 22:12, 27). The political system, seeking to protect the wealth of the increasingly affluent (and thus protecting the source of the politician's wealth and power) will create laws which oppress the people while protecting the powerful (Ezek. 22:23-25). The religious system will then support this political and economic collusion by "blessing" it (for which they will be amply rewarded). This they will do by using their access to God by keeping the people from God, thus creating a religion of control while seeking their own power (Ezek. 22:26). The voices of accountability to that institution—the prophets—will gradually be seduced by money, power and prestige, and thus will be stilled (Ezek. 22:28). The people, oppressed, exploited and controlled by the systems created to serve them, will become the exploiters of each other (Ezek. 22:29-31). Thus, the essential spiritual nature of the nation, city, business, church or family which has been created by God will become irredeemably evil (Ezek. 22:3-12).

Perhaps the most profound analysis of this corrupting power of systems was given by St. Paul. Faced with an increasingly oppressive Rome, Paul promulgated the doctrine of the "principalities and powers." The increasing evil in an institution, Paul taught, is not simply because of the evil that is within humanity. It occurs because the systems are particularly vulnerable to the demonic. Because they deal with the most primal realities of life, the systems can become demonically possessed. The struggle in the nation, city, business, church or family is not simply "against flesh and blood;" instead, it is against "the rulers, the authorities, the powers of this dark world and against the spiritual forces of evil in the heavenly realm" (Eph. 6:10-12). And that is why it is a particularly pervasive and intense battle.

Deeper than its social analysis, the Scriptures are even more concerned about what the people of God—Israel, the remnant, and finally the church—are to do to challenge the corruption of the systems. The essential vocation of the church is to expose the systems for the demonic exploiters of people that they are (Col. 2:11-15) and to work for the transformation of the people and their institutions into the corporate entities God created then to be (Eph. 3:8-12, John 9:1-39, Jer. 22:1-5, 13-17).

What this means, in practical outworking, is that the church is to be on the side of the poor, the oppressed, the exploited. It is to work for their empowerment—both by the gospel and by their own self-determination. Thus the Old Testament Scriptures declare to Israel:

> *Is not this the sort of worship that pleases me—it is the Lord Yahweh who speaks—to break unjust fetters and undo the thongs of the yoke, to let the oppressed go free, and break every yoke, to share your bread with the hungry and shelter the homeless poor (Isa. 58:6-7a)?*

> *I hate and despise your feasts, I take no pleasure in your solemn festivals... But let justice flow like water, and integrity like an unfailing stream (Amos 5:21, 24).*

> *Is there a poor man among you, one of your brothers, in any town of yours in the land that Yahweh your God is giving you? Do not harden your heart or close your hand against that poor brother of yours, but be open-handed with him and lend him enough for his needs... When you give to him, you must give with an open heart; for this Yahweh your God will bless you in all you do and in all your giving (Deut. 15:7-8, 10).*

Because of the overwhelming dominance of the political order by Rome and because of the church's exclusion from the political process, little is said in the New Testament regarding political justice. But the

Christians did have control over their own pocket-books. Therefore, the thrust of the New Testament call to the church regarding the poor is in terms of economic responsibility. Thus, Jesus spoke more about money than any other subject because he perceived money as the most powerful vehicle either to keep a person from God (Luke 18:18-27) or to enhance his relationship with God (Luke 19:1-10). But perhaps the most substantive call to the church to use the power given it (whether economic or spiritual) to work for humanity's liberation is sounded by St. Paul.

The book of Ephesians is about the liberation that comes to humanity through Christ (Eph. 1:3-14; 2:1-22), who defeats both the heavenly principalities and powers and their possession of the systems and structures which drive humanity's institutions (1:15-23; 3:1-13). When the church becomes a body of believers committed to each other's liberation and empowerment in Jesus Christ (4:1-16), this will have a profound impact not only upon each other, but on all society around them. It will radically alter the Christian's life-style into a pure, disciplined life (4:17-23). It will create a body of Christ truly liberating (5:1-20). It will profoundly change the relationships in marriage, empowering the woman (in Paul's day, the legally disenfranchised party) (5:21-33) and protecting defenseless children (6:1-4). It will transform the economic institutions of society, especially protecting the right of the employee (6:5-9). Finally, it will equip the church to engage its city's or nation's political, economic and religious systems in a spiritual warfare that will cause those systems to become what God intended them to be (6:10-17).

The primary way such commitment to the poor is to be lived out by the church is through empowerment. God's people are to practice charity toward the poor (Deut. 15:10-11), are to be concerned about deteriorating human conditions among the poor (Isa. 61:1-9) and are to advocate the cause of the powerless before the systems of power (Jer. 22:13-27). But of far greater emphasis throughout Scripture is the commitment to the self-determination and self-initiative of the poor. Pharaoh could only be faced down by one who cried, "Let my people go." In the Promised Land, debts were to be periodically forgiven so that the poor could undertake the rebuilding of their lives (Deut. 15:7-11), and the corners of a threshed field were not to be harvested so that the poor could gather grain for themselves (Deut. 24:19-22; Ruth 2:1-23). Jeremiah instructed the Israelites enslaved in Babylon to build a life for themselves there (Jer. 29:1-7). Nehemiah called the defeated people of Israel not only to rebuild their own walls (Neh. 2) but also their corporate life (Neh. 8-11). Jesus required the blind man to wash in the Pool of Siloam if he was to receive his sight (John 9); he consistently stated when he healed people, "Your faith has made you whole." Paul stressed that a person's initiative plays a strong role in his salvation; he cannot be helped by God unless he accepts for his own life what God has already provided for him through Christ (Rom. 1:16-17; 12:1-2). The constant theme of Scripture—whether dealing with the liberation of the impoverished powerless or the salvation of the spiritually impoverished—is that of self-initiative, of empowerment through self-determination.

This is why it is biblical for the church to be involved in community organization. The organizing of a community to identify and seek to address their own needs is simply another way of acting out the biblical injunction to "work for your salvation 'in fear and trembling,' for it is God who puts both the will and the action into you" (Phil. 2:13). Participation in community organization provides the church with the most biblically directed and most effective means for bringing about the transformation of a community—through the assumption of responsibility by the community's residents to solve corporately their own problems.

### Self-interest requires it

There is a profound difference between self-interest and selfishness. Selfishness is the seeking of one's own good, irrespective of and often to the exclusion of anyone else's good. Enlightened self-interest, on the other hand, is the seeking of one's good in relation to seeking the good for others. It is the recognition that self-interest is a powerful motivating factor for every person and organization, and to deny that reality in one's self is to deny what it means to be an authentic human being.

People and organizations act out of self-interest. They are concerned about their own effectiveness and success. It is self-interest which drives the compulsion to excel in business or in sports, to achieve the highest objectives, and to be considered by one's peers as a success. It is actually a stronger motivation than the money one gets paid to excel in a job.

What gives self-interest a bad name are those people and organizations who have a compulsion to excel, no matter whom they hurt or what they must do to reach their objectives. When self-interest is no longer enlightened by a concern for the effectiveness of others, then it turns into selfishness and becomes destructive in power.

The same can be said of pride. A measure of self-pride, of respect for one's self, is necessary to provide the motivation one needs to make something of himself. No one appreciates a person who has no sense of his own internal dignity. But when self-respect becomes fixated upon itself, allowing one to develop an exalted opinion of one's self out of proportion to reality, pride becomes odious. It becomes odious, not because pride is bad, but because selfishness is.

A secret of effective community organization is to motivate the people and organizations of a community to discover that it is in the serving of the interests of the community that the interests of each organization is served. In other words, one can more effectively make his organization successful by cooperating in the improvement of the entire life of the community than to seek solely the good of his own organization. This was never so clearly illustrated to me than when I returned to the Chicago neighborhood in which I had done community organizing fifteen years after I had left it to go to Detroit.

As I got off the elevated train and started up Bryn Mawr Avenue, I was astounded by the change. No more trash in the gutters, trees flourishing along the street, new sidewalks (some with brick inlays), businesses obviously thriving, lovely fenced-in lawns where bare ground once lay, apartment buildings sand-blasted, tuck-pointed and freshly painted. My first reaction was, "Gentrification! The rich have pushed out the community's poor and taken over." But I was wrong.

When I stopped by the church I once pastored, and visited with its members, I found out what had happened. The people and organizations of that community—the shops, the businesses, the churches, the poor, the ordinary people—had banded together in that community organization I had helped to found fifteen years earlier. They had set as their top priority the improvement of that community's quality of life. And they had set themselves to that task. The result was the slow, steady upgrading of that community. Each institution, each organization, every individual in that community and their individual self-interests had been served, not by seeking their own good but by organizing together to seek the community's good. That is self-interest operating at its very best.

The church acts out of self-interest. It would deny this, with considerable embarrassment. But to deny it simply means that one does not understand the institutional nature of the church. Institutional needs must always be served, and such service can happen only by self-interest.

Thus, the church is committed to evangelism. But it is as interested in evangelism resulting in the recruitment of new members for that church as it is interested in the salvation of eternal souls. It talks about the spiritual benefit of tithing one's income, but a primary motivation of talking about the tithe is the extra income that tithe represents for the church. Christians might rhapsodize about "worshipping the Lord in the beauty of holiness" but a primary motivation for wanting a good choir and the best preacher possible is to increase Sunday worship attendance.

Christians feel guilty about admitting to such interest. But they should not. They have an institution to run as well as a gospel to proclaim. And an institution requires resources to make it operate successfully. It is in the self-interest of the church to seek to increase its membership, income and worship attendance. And not to admit that is simply to be deluding one's self.

It is in the self-interest of the church to be involved in community organization. For example, people will not come to a church in a trash-filled, graffiti-sprayed neighborhood where muggings regularly occur. It is in the self-interest of the church to join forces with the other groups and people of that community to clean up both the crime and the litter on its streets. By doing so, the church has not only contributed to the welfare of its community. It has also made its building a more desirable place for visitors and members to gather to worship God. It has wisely served its own interests by cooperating with other groups improving that entire community.

It has been clearly demonstrated in both third—and first—world cities that community organization has led to the empowerment of the poor and the improvement of their communities. But that has also led to the strengthening of those churches in such communities, if those churches have participated in that community organization. The wisest thing a church in a deteriorating neighborhood can do—if that church wants to gain members, become strong and maintain its status in that community—is to be active in the organizing of that community to deal with the problems threatening that neighborhood's quality of life. This is enlightened self-interest at its best.

## It can build up the church

In 1972, I wrote a book which showed how my church in Chicago benefitted by applying the principles of community organization to the interior life of the church.[1]

When I came to the Edgewater Presbyterian Church, I found a dispirited, broken people. Getting them to recite their illustrious past (which had been highly effective in addressing the social ills of the neighborhood), I motivated them with the reminder, "We have done it before; we can do it again." I challenged the leadership of the church to determine its own future; 52 of those leaders then gathered every Wednesday night for half a year, studying the Scripture, networking that community, identifying their issues and determining the actions they would take to address those issues. We dealt with the whole life of the church—worship, church school, adult education, pastoral care, visitation, evangelism, community ministries, the use of our 92-room building, the stewardship of our money. The result of that study was a strong sense of direction and determination which drove that congregation for the seven years I pastored that church (and still drives it today).

---

1    *Christian Revolution for Church Renewal* (Philadelphia: Westminster Press, 1972)

The application of community organizing principles to the church can enrich the life of that church. Every principle presented in this book which can contribute to the strengthening of the community can be equally used to strengthen the life of a church. The members of the church can network each other, discovering what each other's issues and concerns are. Coalitions can be formed in the church to address the interior problems of the church as well as community issues; thus, rather than recruiting for a worship committee, the people of the congregation most concerned about worship could gather together to take charge of that church's worship (i.e., analyze the worship issues of that congregation and undertake steps to resolve those issues).

The pedagogy of action and reflection can be as effectively used in the church and its coalitions as it can in a community's coalitions. Organizing these coalitions to set their objectives for the worship, education, pastoral care, outreach, stewardship and building use—and then to carry out those objectives through their own self-determined projects and actions—can place in the hands of the people most concerned the actual organizing of the life of that congregation.

Confrontation can become a means by which church decision-makers wrestle with commonly identified problems. Where there is honest, loving confrontation, there will not be the violence of churches being torn apart.

Leadership can be developed in the church as the coalitions identify budding leadership in their midst and call forth that leadership. If the established leadership of the church has created a mentoring and discipleship-training approach to leadership development, they can take that "budding" leadership under their wings and prepare them for effective church leadership. Participation in the community organization can also be a truly effective way of preparing that budding leadership, as they learn from the community organization how to be an effective leader even as they contribute to it.

Even a convention can be used to restore life and hope to a congregation. A convention can be an effective vehicle to enable the congregation to set objectives, establish priorities and celebrate the life of the church. It was my privilege recently to lead three congregations in a two-day convention they undertook together which seems to be profoundly changing their future. The three congregations are in the same deteriorating Los Angeles community. As we planned for the convention for over nine months, twelve teams of three people representing each church networked and researched the community. At the convention, nearly 75% of the membership of all three churches attended. There, a team presented a report on the networking and research of the community, we celebrated our life together, and shared Bible study in teams from all three churches. Then, meeting in each separate congregation, we prepared mission statements; intriguingly all three were quite similar. With some editing, a mission statement was created, the decision was made to form a mission-oriented parish of the three churches, and objectives were drawn up for that parish. Finally, the next day, we gathered in a celebration which packed the sanctuary of the largest of the church buildings, and the parish was launched.

Of course, the application of community organizing principles to the church will not succeed if the church is not also involved in its community organization. It is involvement in that organization which trains church members for congregational leadership, creates a vision for the church's community ministry through involvement in the community's issues, and which provides the model for organizing the congregation. When the church builds upon its experience in the community organization by using organizing principles in its own interior life, then the life and mission of that church will undergo profound transformation and empowerment.

### It provides a witness to the church's faith

The final reason for the church to be involved in its community organization is an evangelical one. Commitment to community organizing provides the vehicle for the church to effectively witness to its faith in Christ. It carries out that witness in two ways.

First, a community organization has great potential. But that potential can be turned to evil as well as to good. Whenever people gain power, they can use that power for their own self-aggrandizement. And the poor are no less likely to do this than are the rich, for the poor are subject to the same temptations as are the powerful. But if God's people —the church—have really entered into the life of that slum or squatter settlement, if they have identified with the people and worked side-by-side with them in the cause of justice, if they have been willing to undertake the most difficult and risky aspects of that work, if the church and its people give themselves away rather than profit from their involvement, then that church gains a profound credibility in that community. Because of its integrity, its willingness to risk, its freedom to ask the hard questions, its lack of selfishness, the church can become the conscience both of that organization and of the community. The first way the church can witness to its faith is through becoming the body that most shapes the spiritual grounding of that empowering effort.

But there is a second way the church can witness in that community organization. The church that has undertaken that kind of incarnational ministry described in this book and has placed itself on the line with the poor is a church that gains a profound respect from that community. In being willing to lose its life, it saves it. The people of the community will listen to that church, will listen to what it has to say and the gospel it has to proclaim. That slum or squatter settlement knows the church did not have to risk its existence by joining common cause with them. But it did risk and did join and did work. And in return the people will want to know what motivated the church to so commit itself to the people. They will want to hear about a Christ who also incarnated himself in our world, and they will often respond to that Christ. That is why, today throughout the world, the city churches which uniformly most experience growth are churches which are intensely involved in community organization. This is the final reason the church should participate in community organization.

In November 1990, I visited a slum in Mombasa, Kenya. It was a most depressing visit—not because of the squalor of the people as much as because of the naïveté of a humanitarian organization.

An international organization (not World Vision) entered this slum several years ago. They did not like what they saw, so they decided to do something to empower these people. They placed a drainage and sewer system underneath the slum, laid out and asphalted broad streets above the sewer lines, installed electric street lights, and built beautiful school and public buildings. Through their influence, they convinced the government to sell the land upon which each settler had built a shack to that poor squatter for twenty Kenya shillings (about one U.S. dollar). The agency then negotiated with several banks to make loans to these squatters at very generous terms so that these new owners of the land could build sound homes upon that land.

The agency had done all they could do, they thought. They had literally built a modern infrastructure under that community. They had made it possible for every squatter to own his land. And they had provided the means by which each squatter could build adequate, affordable housing for themselves.

The years have passed. And what has happened to that project? The squatters purchased their respective lots with their twenty shillings. Almost all borrowed the money from the bank. But few houses were erected. And soon, the wealthy came into the community, offered the squatters 20,000 Kenyan shillings for each plot and erected upon them grand homes. The poor, now bereft of the only property they ever owned, moved down the road to start another squatter settlement. And the former slum is now in a gentrification transition as it becomes a settlement for the rich.

Were the poor residents of that slum simply irresponsible opportunists? Could they not see the opportunity to own their own home? Were they just helpless victims of the rich?

Not really. It was simply that no one had actually *asked* them what they wanted. That international organization, the government, the banks just assumed that these people would want to be permanent home-owners in that squatter settlement. But the people did not choose this course of action; it was chosen for them. So they rejected it, and simply acted pragmatically on the opportunity afforded them.

As I drove through that Mombasa slum, I could not help but think of other powerless people I have known—the mothers in Natal, Brazil, demanding government milk for their children, the Mexico City women creating their own sewing business, the little old Chicago ladies in tennis shoes demanding the closure of that pornographic book store, the Madras slum dwellers packing the sanitation executive's office until he cleaned up their slum, the Detroit poor building homes and telling the foundation president to "take his money and shove it," the Chicago people confronting the banks over their "red-lining" of their community, the Nairobi churches working with the Mathare Valley poor to build their own sanitation system.

And I was reminded once again of the profound difference between empowering people or simply providing for them. For in each of the successful ventures of empowerment, the people decided what they wanted to do, and acted collectively to solve those problems. Out of such self-determination and respect for the capabilities of the poor does true empowerment flow. For as the Christian apologist Origen wrote to his heathen tormentors:

> [The poor are said to be] the rag, tag and bobtail of humanity. But Jesus does not leave them that way. Out of material you would have thrown away as useless, he fashions [people of strength], giving them back their self-respect, enabling them to stand on their feet and look God in the eye. They were cowed, cringing, broken things. But the Son has set them free!

# BIBLIOGRAPHY

ALINSKY, SAUL. *Reveille for Radicals*. New York: Random House, 1969, $4.95. Originally published in 1946 by the dean of American organizers, *Reveille* is the standard presentation on community organizing.

BOBO, KIMBERLEY. *Lives Matter: A Handbook for Christian Organizing*. Kansas City, MO: Sheed & Ward, 1986, $8.95. While focusing on the issue of hunger, Bobo presents basic philosophy and techniques of community organizing, including the characteristics of effective organizers.

CHAMBERS, ED. "Organizing for Family and Congregation." Huntington, N.Y.: Industrial Areas Foundation, 675 W. Jericho Turnpike, 11743; 1978. This monograph examines in a comprehensive way why the church and community families should be involved in community organizing.

LINTHICUM, ROBERT C. *City of God; City of Satan*. Grand Rapids, MI: Zondervan, 1991, $15.95. This exhaustive urban biblical theology contains in detail the community organizing strategy of Nehemiah mentioned throughout this book.

MAGLAYA, FELIPE E. *Organizing People for Power: A Manual for Organizers*. Asia Committee for People's Organization, 1982. A succinct "how-to" manual for organizing in a Third-World urban context; must reading for pastors and community leaders in Third-World cities. Contained in Simpson's and Stockwell's workbook (see below).

PIERCE, GREGORY F. *Activism that Makes Sense: Congregations and Community Organization*. New York: Paulist Press, 1984, $6.95. An excellent presentation on community organizing philosophy. Pierce's book develops the relationship between the Christian faith, church life and mission and community organization. Must reading for a Christian.

SIMPSON, DICK and STOCKWELL, CLINTON. *Congregations and Community Organizing*. Chicago: ICUIS, 1987, $15.00. A compilation of major articles on community organization, this workbook is an extremely effective introduction to the field because of its unique mixture of historical reflection and practical instruction.

*The Organizer Mailing.* San Francisco: Organize Training Center. The Organize Training Center periodically distributes the *Organizer Mailing,* which is effective in keeping one informed on developments in the field.

All books listed above, except the Linthicum book and the Chambers article, can be ordered from the Institute on the Church in Urban-Industrial Society, 4750 N. Sheridan Rd., Suite 327, Chicago IL 60640; telephone: (312)271-7070 at cost of book plus 10 percent postage and handling. The Organizer Mailer can be ordered for $35.00 per year from the Organize Training Center, 1095 Market Street, #419, San Francisco, CA 94103; (415)552-8990. Chambers' article can be ordered from the Industrial Areas Foundation. Linthicum's book can be ordered from MARC, 919 W. Huntington Dr., Monrovia, CA. 91016; telephone (818)303-8811.